I0390931

About the Author

Kia Davis helps entrepreneurs turn their ideas into reality. Combining corporate strategy experience with a love for entrepreneurs, Kia has developed Flashpoint 100. Now small and medium enterprises (SMEs) can get the kind of results that giant corporations with millions of dollars in resources enjoy.

Flashpoint 100 methods have been used with small business entrepreneurs, tech startups, and portfolio companies of investors. Passionate about providing an environment for small businesses to thrive, Kia has also worked with governments, NGOs, and innovation agencies to design ecosystems around the world.

Kia's work in growth and entrepreneurship has led her to projects in countries as diverse as Colombia, Dubai, Ecuador, Ireland, Kenya, the Netherlands, Switzerland, Tanzania, the United Kingdom, and the United States. Kia holds a BA in consumer psychology from Yale University and an MBA from Insead in France/Singapore.

Kia can be reached at <u>Kiardavis@Flashpoint100.com</u>.

FLASH point 100

FLASH point 100

radical business growth in 100 days

Kia Davis

Table of Contents

⋐ ❖ ⋑

Acknowledgements

I would like to thank the many people who helped with the ideas, research, content, writing, and editing of this book. First and foremost I'd like to thank my mother, Dr. Billie Ann Davis, my biggest inspiration and cheerleader. I'd also like to thank the uber-mentor and tireless supporter of entrepreneurs, Scott Gillespie. Other people who have invited me to join their growth efforts or lent their extraordinary intelligence, business acumen, support, and feedback include Martin Acosta, Amy Bonsall, Steve Cronin, Nina Curley, Star Davis, Tarig El-Sheikh, Kali Ferguson, Swati Khanna, Gaurav Khemani, John Purkiss, Ritesh Tilani, Rajal Upadhyaya, and Matt Wilson.

Several companies, investors, companies, and groups I've worked with over the years have been instrumental to my understanding of how entrepreneurs work their magic, such as Anthemis Group, GIST, the Insead Global Entrepreneurship Club, Jigsaw Group, T2 VC, and Technoserve.

Special thanks to Lee Ann at FirstEditing.com, my talented and speedy editor for this book edition. Any errors in the text are entirely my own. Also thanks to graphic designers Kusmin at JPKusmin@gmail.com and Miladinka Milic of www.milagraphicartist.com. Your work was transformative.

Flashpoint

/flaSHpoint/

Noun.

1. The critical point at which something causes a major or significant action.

2. The lowest temperature at which the vapor above a liquid ignites by flame.

൪❖൭

Glossary

Asset: Anything a company owns that gives it value, such as property, machines, trademarks, patents, etc.

Baseline performance: The starting point for company performance, before Flashpoint 100. For example, last year's revenue and profit.

Capacity: The maximum amount of a good or service a company can produce based on existing assets and people.

Capital allocation: How financial resources are assigned to give the best return, usually based on money, time, and risk.

Capital expenditure (capex): Investments into property, equipment, or things that make a company more valuable overall.

Checkpoint: A meeting every three weeks to review progress on projects and decide resourcing or cancellation.

Company diagnostic: A 1-page tool that reviews how well a company is doing so you can compare progress.

Company values: Shared beliefs that provide guidance on how employees interact and behave, like transparency, honesty, fairness, sustainability, diversity, etc.

Conversion metrics: Ways to convert different financial numbers such as revenue, customers, or costs, to profit.

Cost of sales: The cost to produce or develop your products and services, but not including overheads.

Dashboard: the number of projects in process, their status, the current amount spent, and the remaining amount to be allocated.

Earnings: Profit before project costs.

Game-Changer projects: High-impact, long-term projects that are tested for feedback in a low-cost way.

Housekeeping projects: Projects that make the company more professional overall, but that might have no impact on profit.

Low-Hanging Fruit projects: Projects that are easy to execute and deliver benefits immediately.

Meat and Potatoes projects: Projects that take 100 days or less to implement, and which deliver lasting results over time.

Mission statement: A statement that outlines how the vision will be achieved, including where the company will strive for excellence.

Monitoring: Tracking progress on projects.

Net profit: Profit after project costs.

Operating expenditure (opex): Ongoing expenses for the company to do business, such as rent, salaries, inventory, or marketing costs.

Project: An idea ready to be executed, complete with timing, costs, objectives, and action owners.

Project champion: The person responsible for overseeing a project's execution.

Pulse Check: A weekly meeting to monitor project performance.

Resource allocation: Deciding how much money to invest in different projects and ideas.

Resources: Anything the company has access to that's limited, such as money, time, and assets.

Revenue: The amount of money that a company receives for what it sells.

Tinderbox: The project portfolio.

Vision statement: A short, one-sentence description of a company's ambition or identity.

Working capital: The unavailable funds due to timing differences between payments from customers and payments to suppliers/others.

Introduction

When it comes to your business, you're all in. Your savings, several years of your life, your professional and personal reputation; everything has been sunk into your business, and the business must work.

In the time since you've started it, nothing has gone as planned. It took time to get the permits and set up the office, several rounds of employees, a painful period when you didn't know how you'd pay the bills, and those few months when you were within spitting distance of bankruptcy. You fought tooth and nail for the first customer, and for the next ones after that. You were disappointed by employees and friends. You faced broken promises from customers, suppliers, partners, and even the government. A handful of people among family and friends took a chance and invested in your dream.

Finally, things have eased up. You breathe better. You sleep better. The bills get paid on time. Employees get paid on time. Customers pay on time. Suppliers deliver on time. There are still problems here and there, of course, but the business is becoming a well-oiled machine. And though the hours are still long, now you know how to deliver to your customers, how to manage your inventory and finances, how to keep the lights on, which employees to hire, how to pay them on time, and when to let them go. You're also managing dozens of other miracles that seemed impossible when you started.

Lately, there's been a catch in your voice whenever you describe your business. That old familiar ache in the belly—the one you thought you had said good-bye to long ago—is back. It's the ache of doing it again, pulling the rabbit out of the hat to build and grow something new and special. You begin to ask yourself:

WHAT'S NEXT?

It's time for something new. You are more confident and knowledgeable than when you first started; however, you'll need a new set of skills for the next set of challenges. It's time to reinvent yourself, breathe new life into the business, and take it to the next level—again. You know that you can make a big impact, if only you had the time or money. Your desk drawer is overflowing with new ideas scribbled on bits of paper. Many of them would work, but between running your business and finally getting a good night's sleep, it's hard to see how to put them into practice.

The skill set you need includes finding new opportunities, choosing the ones that are worth it, investing in them, and developing a plan of action. It also involves checking and rechecking progress, asking employees to do things in a brand-new way, and seeing it through to the end. By focusing your efforts in a short burst of intense activity, you can get the most out of your employees, see what works and what doesn't, and get results early on.

Going all-out for a short period of time requires focus, dedication, good decision making, and a smart use of resources. You will need to monitor how you spend your time as much as how you spend your money. The ultimate mark of success is whether you get results, and those results come as a result of hard work and smart choices.

What If You Could Be a Personal Trainer for Your Business?

If you were overweight and wanted to slim down, you might hire a personal trainer. She would help you work out so you can achieve a smaller waistline and bigger muscles. Her main tools would be goal-setting, inspiration, motivation, and technical knowledge. However, you would still have to do the work yourself. You couldn't phone it in. If you skipped a day of working out, you skipped a day of results.

As scary as she might be, a gruff trainer who terrifies you into doing one more push-up, one more minute on the treadmill, and one more crunch, is priceless. While personal trainers have deep knowledge of their field, their knowledge is meaningless if you're not willing to put in the work. Their real value is in helping you actually *do* it.

Like people, companies also benefit from a period of getting into shape and becoming stronger, more sustainable, bigger, and more efficient. Their "personal trainers" could be internal champions, new investors, or external consultants. As an entrepreneur, you're an ideal candidate to be the personal trainer for your business; as a lead decision maker, you can work within the company to find and fix problems, identify opportunities, implement ideas, and measure progress. You can inspire, motivate, and help plan with the team, but you need commitment and hard work to come from all levels. Employees, suppliers, customers, investors, directors, and other stakeholders all have a role to play in getting the work done.

What Will You Get out of Flashpoint 100?

You already know the types of ideas that you would pursue, given enough time and money. This book will give you the skills to turn those ideas into reality—without breaking the bank. This book will give you the necessary tools so that at each step along the way, you are making decisions and getting fast feedback on how well things are going. This book is also designed to help you empower, motivate, and get the best from your employees and other supporters.

Ultimately, this book will help you to grow your business, achieve big results, and make your wildest dreams a reality.

Who Should Read this Book?

This book is relevant if you are a business owner, entrepreneur, or general manager of a small business. Your core business is going well, but you are looking for new challenges to transform and grow the company. You have the fire and desire to go through a process of renewal, transformation, and growth, and you are willing to put yourself and your employees through extraordinary measures to achieve it. You can devote several months to intense activity and experimentation, and you have cash in the bank to invest in worthy projects and plans. You are willing to be disciplined in your implementation and spending. You are courageous enough to communicate all this to your employees, and influential enough to gain their support.

Flashpoint 100 has been developed for the smaller, more nimble company that has a lot to gain (and little to lose) by starting on a path of growth and transformation. Though many corporate executives could benefit from the methods in this book, most large companies struggle with quick decision making and rapid innovation. Market leaders often find it difficult to gamble on new and innovative measures if the core business might be threatened. If you are a manager, owner, or decision maker who is in a position to make these decisions, be ready to think big!

Similarly, this book is not written for very young startups. Success for these companies takes a different type of soul-searching and trial and error to get the product just right for the first customers. There are plenty of books on getting started that detail the biggest priorities of developing the initial idea into a product, getting set up, and getting the first sales. This book is not designed to help with these important issues.

What Benefits Should You Expect from this Book?

Great effort produces great results. Flashpoint 100 is intense and will help you transform your business. Just like a major house renovation, things look ugly and messy for a while before the house is revamped and renewed, becoming more beautiful. Similarly, Flashpoint 100 also generates value: revenue increases, profit improvements, process efficiencies, and clarity surrounding the strategic direction of your business. Long-term expansion and growth plans will become clear. Medium-term plans of brand development and sales improvement will get executed. Short-term plans yield a bump in revenues or cost savings, greater profit margins, and solved problems. Underlying all of this are improvements in the professionalism, communication, and management of your company, giving it staying power and making it a great place to work.

While the program isn't long, the results are long-lasting. Flashpoint 100 is designed to give you an immediate revenue increase within four months and at least 100 percent revenue increase within three years. The exact outcome will depend on the current size of your company, the length of your sales cycle, and the specific projects you choose to implement. Some companies will double their revenues every year, while others may take even longer than three years to do so. Following the path of the book, you should expect:

- **Within 30 days**: There is a shared knowledge of the biggest problems and opportunities in the company. Tiny, ongoing problems are fixed.

- **Within 60 days**: Revenue increases come from early improvements in sales or marketing, along with cost improvements due to changes in processes or negotiated discounts.

- **Within 100 days**: Longstanding issues are fixed, new processes improve professionalism, revenues increase from sales and marketing improvements, and cost savings are gained from supplier and process changes.

- **Within 1 year**: Revenues and profit are improved, there is higher customer retention, it costs less per-unit to make your product(s) and/or service(s), and major new growth and expansion initiatives are in place (for customers, markets, products, or brands).

- **Within 3 years**: New products, services, markets, or brands have doubled or tripled revenues and profit, there's a significant increase in customer numbers and sales, and increased capacity.

Exact results will vary, but if you have the willingness and determination to embark on a path of business transformation, results will follow.

How to Read this Book

Flashpoint 100 is a step-by-step guide to achieving rapid and lasting growth in your business. It will help you identify issues, build projects, execute plans, and invest in the right things. You will assemble and execute a portfolio of projects (the tinderbox) and monitor progress so you know what's working. You will also make sure that your resources are spent efficiently.

To help you keep track of the strict timelines for Flashpoint 100, each chapter tells you the days that each activity should take.

Along the way, 'Scenarios' are highlighted showing case examples, many of which are real examples from companies the author has worked with.

This book has been written in American English and references the US dollar, but this is only because it's a widely understood currency. Flashpoint 100 has been used all over the world, and works especially well in emerging markets.

If you have very little time, read Flashpoint 100 At a Glance (Chapter 1) and Flashpoint 100 Fundamentals (Chapter 3) to get an idea of how Flashpoint 100 works.

Templates at the back of the book will help you keep track of your notes and numbers. For online templates and support on Flashpoint 100, visit www.flashpoint100.com.

A glossary is also included at the front that gives definitions for terms that are used frequently in the book.

PART 1

WHAT IS FLASHPOINT 100?

The common question asked in business is, 'why?' That's a good question, but an equally valid question is, why not?

— Jeff Bezos, CEO of Amazon.com

Chapter 1
Flashpoint 100 At a Glance

Flashpoint 100 is summarized here so you can get a feel and flavor for it before starting. If you don't have time to implement the full program, read this summary and the following section so that you can improvise. The sections that follow give detailed information about Flashpoint 100 and how to execute it.

Flashpoint 100 is a 100-day plan to identify new ideas and fast-track them with customers and in the company, so that you know what works and what doesn't. Flashpoint 100 relies on fast identification and execution of ideas via trial and error. After agreeing on a vision and a key overriding objective, a large number of projects are started, monitored, and cancelled based on how well they match up to your expectations. Each project has clear goals and milestones (markers of progress), and project costs are doled out as you reach different milestones. In the end, projects that are more successful are completed and given full investment to roll out further. This limits the downside and maximizes the potential benefit.

The ultimate goal is to complete a mix of projects within 100 days that immediately grow the business and set it on a path to permanent growth.

The Phases of Flashpoint 100

- **Gather your Kindling: 4 days**—Agreeing on the company vision and ultimate goal (super-objective), choosing company values, interviewing stakeholders on opportunity areas.
- **Strike: 10 days**—Brainstorming, turning ideas into plans, planning projects, and making the final project selection.
- **Heat: 81 days**—Implementing projects, reviewing individual projects weekly, reviewing the project portfolio every three weeks, investing in projects as they meet their milestones, keeping employees motivated and engaged.
- **Ignite: 5 days**—Analyzing performance and benefits, deciding which long-term bets to take forward.

What Makes Flashpoint 100 Successful?

Flashpoint 100 has several elements that make it distinct, and these elements are carefully selected for the way they work together to turn ideas into reality, and achieve profit growth in a cost-effective way:

- **Using what works**—Relying on input from existing customers, suppliers, investors, and other stakeholders to get better and new ideas, and test new plans.
- **Experimentation**—Trying new things, checking what works, and making corrections where necessary.
- **Artful resource allocation**—Selectively making investments as projects deserve them.

- **Balanced tinderbox of projects**—Mixing short- and long-, high- and low-impact projects.
- **Rewards, recognition, and fun**—Creating a fun culture that rewards energy, accomplishments, and creativity.
- **Trust and empowerment**—Inspiring employees to take ownership of projects, make key decisions, and trust that they won't be punished for things going off-plan. Assigning project leads from junior to senior levels.
- **Transparency and communication**—Being transparent and clear about the purpose and progress of Flashpoint 100, including roles and expected benefits and results.

Types of Projects and Their Benefits

- **Game-Changer Ideas**—High-impact, long-term projects that are tested for feedback in a low-cost way. These give clarity to which big new idea(s) will be successful in the market, and how to implement and finance them.
- **Meat & Potatoes** —Projects that take 100 days or less to implement and deliver lasting results over time. These increase revenues from top customers, markets, product lines, or offices.
- **Low-Hanging Fruit**—Projects that are easy to execute and deliver benefits immediately. These create a bump in revenue or profit by executing projects that deliver quick wins
- **Housekeeping** —Areas that make the company more professional overall, but that might have no impact on profit. They fix longstanding issues or make the company more professional and sustainable.

Timing

Flashpoint 100 takes 100 days from start to finish. Keeping this deadline is important because 100 days is the amount of time that most people can devote to doing something intensely. Slipping too much on this range risks people losing motivation, and the program risks going uncompleted. The chart below shows which activities happen when, breaking down the 100 days into the key parts. M=Month, D=Day.

Timeline for Flashpoint 100

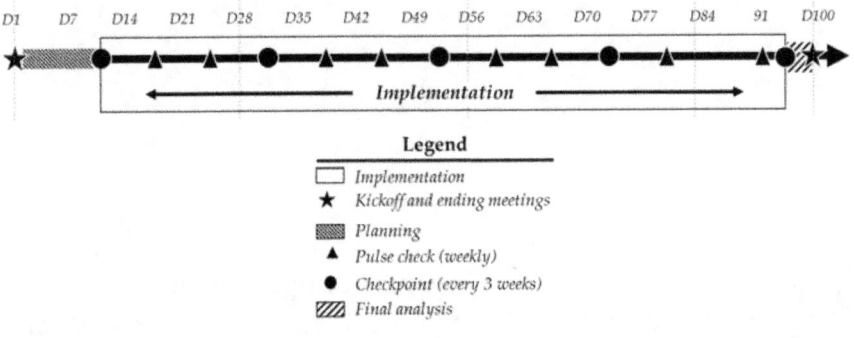

❦ ❖ ❧

Chapter 2
How Large and
Small Businesses Grow

B oth large and small companies struggle with how to grow profitably and make their businesses stronger and more viable. Larger companies might use management consultants to help them form long-term plans for growth. These consultants are hired for their ability to analyze the market for new opportunities, develop solutions to tough problems, and give good plans for pursuing solutions. These plans describe exactly what will happen, when, for how much, and for what benefit.

Once a small business has achieved profitability and the company is running smoothly, entrepreneurs look for ways to get bigger and more profitable. Some companies will go through a major transformation all at once, while others will make changes little by little. Few have the resources or desire to hire expensive management consultants, so they rely on internal resources and immediate opportunities.

The Typical Corporate Strategy Process

Traditional corporate strategy projects by management consultants rely on a flow of good information about the competition, customers, suppliers, and products. Strategy consultants use every tool at their disposal, including their own and others' expertise and published research. A large amount of information is produced about the company and its target market and competitors. This information is then used to formulate a long-term plan, with details on the amount to spend, the number of people to hire, types of activities to do, the forecasted benefits, and the length of time it will take. Monitoring and metrics are chosen to help the company stay on track through the following months and years. The ultimate goal is often a successful execution of a major new idea (such as a merger) or a major growth push (such as doubling the stock price in five years).

A corporate strategy plan might include a number of projects related to decreasing costs, improving marketing, launching new products, or entering new markets. The plans might outline purchasing companies, building new factories, forming new partnerships, targeting new types of customers, relocating offices, or changing the pricing structure.

The Typical Small Business Strategy Process

Small businesses use a different process than their larger counterparts; usually one that is less rigorous, less structured, and is more reliant on readily available resources. Many business owners take opportunities as they come, such as deciding whether or not to buy a competitor or launch a new product. These entrepreneurs typically rely on a mixture of gut feeling, currently available opportunities, current cash flow, and trial and error to decide on new things to do. They also have a very good long-term vision and are great at making sure opportunities that come up help them get to where they want to be.

Unlike large companies, small business entrepreneurs can focus more on balancing long-term ambitions with short-term needs. The deep business knowledge that successful entrepreneurs have allows them to make informed decisions about where to make new investments and how to develop the business. While many large companies suffer from slow decision making due to the number of people in the company, smaller firms can execute projects relatively quickly.

Key Differences between Corporate Strategy and Flashpoint 100

This book bridges the gap between the two processes, giving small businesses the benefit of a structured program of activities aimed at big results, without the large investment of time and money required for major strategy consulting firms.

Flashpoint 100 has some major differences to a major corporate strategy project:

- *No cherry-picking winners*—In Flashpoint 100, winners are not picked up-front. Anything that could be beneficial is attempted. Nothing is discarded until there is a good reason. Everything that is feasible and shows real possibility gets added to the list of options.
- *Internal analysis*—Flashpoint 100 relies on the intuition and knowledge of management and others, like employees and customers. There is little need to get published industry reports or deep market analysis. Most entrepreneurs know exactly what they would do given enough time and money, but they lack a method to identify and prioritize their ideas so that the best ones get done first.
- *Trial and error*—To find the best projects, all good ideas are given a fair chance to succeed in the marketplace. Prototypes, tests, trials, and market experiments are all cost-efficient ways to test ideas. Following market feedback, only the best ideas make it through to full implementation. Choosing performance hurdles up-front helps you make the decision later on. This could create a small amount of wasted effort and money initially, but saves much larger amounts of wasted effort and money on products and ideas that will not work.

The difference between corporate strategy and Flashpoint 100

Traditional corporate strategy	Flashpoint 100
Ideas from market analysis	Ideas from management, employees, others
Final plans are selected internally by company	Final plans are determined by market, customers
Market analysis	Market validation
Optimization	Upside
Expensive	Cost-efficient
3-month initial analysis	2-week initial analysis
External consultants	Internal champions
Benefits realized in long-term	Benefits realized immediately

What's Critical for Small Businesses?

Small businesses need to remain flexible, dynamic, nimble, and efficient. Rarely can they afford to splash out on something expensive and then wait to see whether or not it works. Results need to be felt immediately so leaders can course-correct where necessary. In contrast, large companies often make bets that are years into the future; but they also have the cushion of knowing that if it doesn't work out, it won't affect most of their operations. Small companies don't have this luxury. Many entrepreneurs make decisions instinctively, knowing what's right without doing a lot of thinking and analysis. Doing this successfully comes with experience, time, and a deep knowledge of the business.

Getting it Right the First Time vs. Trial and Error

Big companies might go through a rigorous process to identify the next big thing, such as a new product or entering a new market. Usually this involves spending a lot of time perfecting the product, then a lot of time marketing it. Despite careful thinking and a dedicated process, even products from the biggest companies fail. However, a program of trial and error, coupled with a limited budget, allows a business to get early and cheap feedback on whether or not the product can be successful. This way, when the product launches, it has a better chance of success, and you can enjoy "happy accidents."

While experimentation is great, it's important not to spend too much money on too many things without knowing the goal in advance. And by being conservative with up-front payouts, you can get feedback on what's working and make necessary changes before committing significant investment.

Upside vs. Downside

Small businesses work very hard just to keep the lights on. In the beginning, each day can feel like a fight to the death: every decision is important and could spell success or disaster. However, even in these times, smaller companies have more to gain than to lose. Market leaders aren't in the same position; being at the top is a privilege that few companies have, and they can't afford to lose it by rocking the boat too much. In his book *The Innovator's Dilemma*,[1] Clay Christensen discusses how big companies find it very difficult to innovate the way small companies can. For big corporations, it's too easy to keep riding the coattails of their own success instead of finding ways to transform themselves. Meanwhile, their smaller competitors with nothing to lose are finding game-changing ways of entering the market. Ultimately, this widening difference leads to the downfall of the market leaders.

Small companies have more upside (potential for success) than downside (potential for disaster). Many could double, triple, or quadruple, and still have plenty of room to grow. This puts them in a great position to experiment. Since there are so many opportunities, by trying a wide range of ideas they are likely to stumble upon a number of concepts that will work and can make a big difference.

---

[1] Christensen, Clayton M. *The Innovator's Dilemma: When New Technologies Cause Great Firms to Fail*. Boston, MA: Harvard Business School Press, 1997.

The Right Place for Market Research

For most large corporations, market research is a staple of developing long-term strategies, testing new product ideas, and monitoring the company's brand with customers. Market research can be incredibly valuable. It can also be expensive, time-consuming, and a waste of time. Many market research agencies require significant effort by the client company to properly conduct a market research project. Often a full-time employee is responsible to develop the overall objectives, input into the project design, manage the agency, and interpret the results. In order to get a good outcome, agencies need to understand your business (to know which questions to ask), understand your customer (to know the best way to ask the questions), and understand what you are looking for (to know what a good result looks like). With poor design, survey respondents may embrace or reject a new product without properly understanding it, and companies end up with thousands of useless data points. A close relationship with a market research agency can help prevent these mistakes, but this takes time and effort.

Few small companies have the time, patience, money, or staff to properly manage an in-depth market research campaign. That's why it's essential to aim every effort at a specific outcome. Many small businesses can get good results by turning to the experts at their fingertips: their customers and employees. A rigorous review of customer needs and a moderate amount of desktop research should reveal a lot of useful information. Few small businesses need to know the size of the entire market anyway—they have so much room to grow before it matters! Market research can be great for areas that require in-depth analysis, such as consumer habits and media preferences.

Get the Right People Involved

When a company is just starting out, the excitement is palpable, the company is humming, and there is a lot to do just to get it off the ground. After a while, the enthusiasm may decline as things start running on their own and challenges fade into more mundane tasks. After a long period of time, working at even the best-run company can become a chore. Sometimes, this can lead to complacency and boredom. While people may be quite happy with their jobs, the daily grind of a well-run company may lose some of the early excitement.

However, there are ways to breathe new life into a company. Creating a new campaign for people to participate in is one option. As people work together in new teams, on new projects, and face new challenges, the initial sense of excitement and enthusiasm can return. Ambitious and motivated employees can have a new sense of control over projects, creating more interest in long-term career options and creating a stronger sense of loyalty.

There is a catch, however. People cannot usually sustain high-energy periods for a long time. Eventually they need a break to recover and rejuvenate. This is why Flashpoint 100 is only 100 days long; that's about how long people can work at an intense pace before they start feeling burnt out. This length of time also fits neatly with quarterly business calendars; you can begin the process in one quarter and begin seeing results in the next. For businesses that have a board of directors (or investors) that meet quarterly, involving them in the process prepares them for requests involving major changes or additional investment during the next meeting. Impressing them with achievements is a great way to convince them to approve investment requests.

By creating a hard deadline of 100 days, it's easier to ask employees and others to go all out to get things done, and gives people the motivation to work harder. Other bonuses like incentives, rewards, and recognition keep it running smoothly; people appreciate recognition for their hard work, and this makes them want to continue working hard.

Create a Sense of Fun

Flashpoint 100 is hard work, but it is also very rewarding. Your employees will be spending a lot of time doing new things, solving new problems, and creating new opportunities. This is easier to do in an environment that is upbeat, energetic, and fun. Doing what you can to create this atmosphere shows appreciation to the employees, and supports the hard work that you expect of them.

A fun environment can be created in different ways. Remember, the aim is to lighten the mood and make people happy to be there. Technology companies like Google are famous for making work fun by offering food, massages, and game rooms. The British company Workshop even installed a slide for people to get to lower floors. But small businesses don't have to offer such dramatic features: surprises, gifts, parties, and competitions can create major effects on a small budget.

Build Trust

Good communication is important during Flashpoint 100. Things move quickly, mistakes get made, and a lot of projects may need additional support. It's critical that you and your team trust each other to highlight issues as they arise, and accomplish projects to the best of everyone's ability. Employees should feel safe enough to point out a problem or a project that is not going well without being blamed. They need to know that no matter what, you believe in them and in what they are doing. This can happen without compromising a culture of accountability in which people are responsible for their actions and outcomes.

Believing in your employees and their abilities really helps this along. Most employees are genuinely interested in doing a good job, and being in charge of something. By allowing them to manage their own work, you are showing them that they are important to the overall effort, and that you have a lot of faith in their ability to get things done. You may even be surprised by how well your employees rise to the challenge. Try not to give the impression that you are using Flashpoint 100 to evaluate their performance, but instead encourage them to take informed risks and experiment.

⊰ ❖ ⊱

Chapter 3
The Flashpoint 100 Fundamentals

lashpoint 100 is a proven method of accomplishing big goals in a timely, cost-efficient way. The process has been developed from years of experience by the author, as well as academic study. Flashpoint 100 uses best practices from fields as wide as social psychology and influence, corporate strategy, investing, decision science theory, pharmaceutical drug development, strategic planning, marketing, food manufacturing, non-governmental organizations (NGOs), international development, and others.

In addition to these fields, two books outline business philosophies consistent with Flashpoint 100. *The Lean Startup*[2] by Eric Ries offers a methodology for software development that relies on early customer feedback, prototyping, rapid iterations, and minimal up-front costs. Nassim Nicholas Taleb's *Antifragile*[3] explores the dynamics of systems

---

[2] Ries, Eric. *The Lean Startup: How Today's Entrepreneurs Use Continuous Innovation to Create Radically Successful Businesses.* Crown Business, 2011.
[3] Taleb, Nassim Nicholas. *Antifragile: Things That Gain from Disorder.* Random House Trade Paperbacks, 2014.

that have more upside than downside, and that benefit from change and happy accidents. These two books showcase the spirit and philosophy of Flashpoint 100.

The goal of Flashpoint 100 is to help you achieve a lot within a short period of time. If you find that you can't follow Flashpoint 100 as it's been laid out, return to this section and improvise while keeping to the governing principles. The secrets to success are straightforward but require sustained focus:

- *Choosing objectives*—Understanding what you want to achieve, how you want to achieve it, and not straying from the goals.
- *Finding Innovative and Creative Solutions*—Finding creative ways to solve problems and create new opportunities.
- *Project Selection and Management*—Turning ideas into actionable plans.
- *Assigning Resources to Projects*—Being cost-effective and maximizing the value you get on everything you spend.
- *Staying Motivated*—Keeping the intensity and helping employees do the same.

Return to these principles when times are tough to help keep Flashpoint 100 on track.

Choosing Objectives

Many business owners start out assuming that everyone in the company agrees on what needs to be done: more sales, lower costs, more customers, more locations, and greater productivity. But few entrepreneurs take the time to decide which ones are most important. This lack of clarity can cause confusion, as people are unable to make trade-offs, work together properly, or ensure that they are tackling the most important areas.

The importance of setting goals and finding objectives is to understand and agree on *why* you are doing something. For a program of activity as intense and rich as Flashpoint 100, it's important to have a goal that acts as a guiding principle. This goal functions like a North Star to keep you oriented and guide your activities to make sure you end up where you want to.

The super-objective is the driving force, the compass, and the engine behind the company. It reflects where you want the company to be in three years, and must be easily understood. Apart from the super-objective, other objectives will help you select and measure specific projects that help you achieve the super-objective and translate it to specific parts of your business. Even when specific projects fail or get changed, you can always ask yourself, how will this affect the objectives? How will this affect achieving the super-objective?

Documents such as the Vision Statement, Mission Statement, and Company Values represent what the business stands for and provides the backbone for Flashpoint 100. If you already have these statements created for the business, this is a good time to review them to see what to fix, add, or change. Ask yourself where you have gotten off track. What no longer makes sense? Which areas have been overlooked for more exciting opportunities or an easier way to do things? Is it better to change these documents, or the way that you do business?

Secrets of Choosing Good Objectives

The biggest trick of choosing objectives is making sure they are clear and measurable, so that monitoring them is straightforward.
- Keep objectives specific and measureable
- Include easy-to-measure quantitative objectives
- Make sure qualitative objectives are descriptive and easy to understand

Keep objectives specific and measurable—Make sure people have a shared understanding of what objectives mean. This is true regardless of whether the objective is quantitative (numerical) or qualitative (descriptive). Non-specific objectives can create confusion, or worse, allow people to game the system. For instance, a goal phrased as "improve order delivery times" could mean "on average", "once in a while", or "by a small amount". Alternatively, "improve order delivery times to three days on average" gives a clear signal on qualifications for success.

Easy-to-measure quantitative objectives — State quantitative objectives in a way that makes them easy to check. This makes it a simple process to see whether they have been met. Avoid quantifiable goals that are difficult to measure. For instance, market share is difficult to measure without a market research agency doing a large and expensive review. However, units sold is easy to measure using readily available information. Quantifiable goals should be measurable on a monthly basis, or on a quarterly basis at a minimum. Good examples of quantitative goals include the number of annual customer subscriptions, the number of units sold in a month, or the overdraft interest paid to the bank. If measurement requires an external party, or an extensive customer survey, or is expensive and time-consuming, avoid it. Find objectives that can be measured with internal information.

Descriptive qualitative objectives — Qualitative objectives don't contain numbers, but should be as descriptive as possible so that different people share an understanding of their meaning. For example, words like *best* or *greatest* don't say much about how to distinguish success from failure. To one person, *best* may mean "cheapest," while to another it may mean "high quality." Choose words that carry a specific meaning, and avoid words that have multiple interpretations. One test is to imagine five different people evaluating a situation. How similar would their assessment be? Some good examples might be goals around transparency, fairness, openness, collaboration, precision, customer focus, or fun. For example, using the five-people-in-a-room test, five people assessing Disney World would probably agree it does a good job of its stated objective to be "the most fun place on earth."

Putting it into Action

Good objectives match your vision. If you see yourself as a top architecture firm that delivers highly functional and highly aesthetic designs, then your objectives might reflect functionality and aesthetics. If you believe that you deliver value by giving good value for the money, then your objectives might include lowering your cost base and focusing on what clients value most.

A good super-objective will not only align with the Vision Statement, but will also reflect where you want to be in three, five, or even ten years.

Apart from the super-objective, junior objectives help progress toward the super-objective. If you are not sure how to find them, try doing a driver-tree. A driver-tree takes a single concept or component and splits it into smaller parts, which are split yet again. See below for a driver-tree on revenues for a sunglass manufacturing business.

Scenario:
Your company sells sunglasses. There are four main types of sunglasses, each with a different price. You decide to analyze the revenues, taking into account customer buying history and the different prices. Starting with the total revenue, you break it down further using a diagram that identifies all the components that drive revenue:

Revenue Driver-Tree

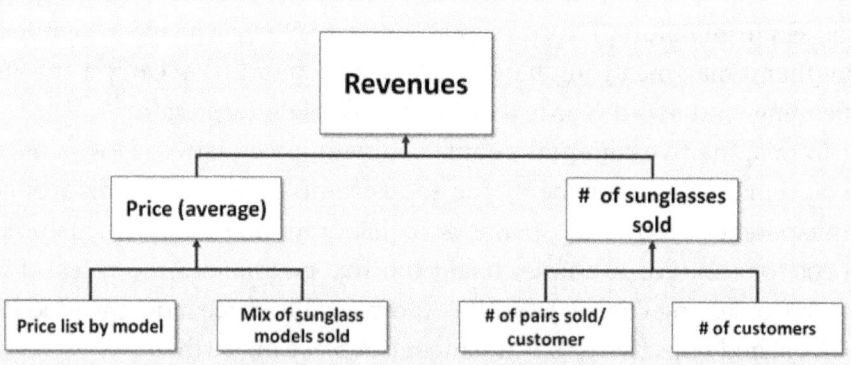

Revenues are driven by the average price multiplied by the number of sunglasses sold. The average price is a function of the different prices for each model, and the mix of models sold. The number of sunglasses sold is a function of the average number of pairs bought by each customer, and the total number of customers.

In this case, revenues are driven by the price list, the mix of models sold, the number of pairs bought by each customer, and the number of customers. Any of these four areas could be good junior objectives. Good junior objectives might be raising the proportion of high-value glasses sold, or increasing the number of glasses that each customer buys.

Try to identify goals that match these criteria:
- Quantitative (numerical) only if they are measureable
- Qualitative if they are specific, and can pass the five-people-in-a-room test
- Aligned to the super-objective, the vision, and identity of the business

Balance different types of objectives so that the mixture reflects what you are trying to achieve overall.

Make the super-objective and junior objectives significant enough to show the health of the business overall, and progress of the projects. Having too many means that you risk managing an overwhelming amount of data. Having too few runs the risk of not reaching the super-objective. To achieve the right number, consider brainstorming a long list of junior objectives, then choose the top five, and see whether any overlap. Select measures that are easy to track and monitor, such as data that can be quickly pulled from accounting software, banking statements, inventory management systems, or CRM (customer relationship management) systems. The aim is to identify a list of meaningful objectives that are relatively easy to track and manage.

Finding Innovative and Creative Solutions

Great results from Flashpoint 100 can be achieved by being as creative as possible, while also staying diligent and practical. This combination is a powerful way to do more with less, to get to an answer that solves multiple problems, and to discover an unusual solution.

Most people assume that creativity is about coming up with something new and different on the spot. But that's not usually how the most creative ideas happen; professional artists and inventors often apply a concept from one field to another, then tinker until it's just right.

Another creativity myth is that epiphanies happen suddenly. In fact, most creatives take a long time to study and experiment. What looks like an "aha moment" often follows years of hard work studying methods, styles, and other artistic geniuses. So when artists encounter a new form that's exciting, they can immediately visualize where and how it fits into their work.

Not just for artists and inventors, creativity is essential for problem-solving and finding new opportunities in business. Fresh thinking and simple creativity can challenge the status quo and take the company in a new direction. Often it's as simple as doing something in a new way, or re-evaluating why things are done the way they are.

Dynamic companies are quite good at this. They stay flexible, adjusting their course as they get good feedback and information. Some start testing product ideas very early on in the process, developing a single prototype from a 3-D printer or "wireframe" (sketch drawing of a website). This allows the company to get opinions and feedback before going through the expensive and time-consuming process of developing the final version.

Innovation is sometimes referred to as "the art of failure." This is a perfect way to describe the experimentation, pain, waste, and trial and error necessary to turn an idea into a new product. Few people realize that great innovations can take years and years of painstaking effort to get a simple result. The pharmaceutical industry is a great example of how innovations happen: the average drug takes over eight years to develop and costs more than $4 billion.[4] Tens of thousands of biological molecules are screened, then years of trials and FDA certifications follow before eventually a single drug emerges. The pharmaceutical industry is unique in how much time is needed to develop an innovation; however, several industries use trial and error to perfect their product development.

Secrets of Innovation and Creativity

Secrets of innovation and creativity center on freeing your mind to find new ways to do things, then experimenting.

- Brainstorm, experiment, and play around
- Use visualization
- Think beyond the box
- Create prototypes and examples

Brainstorm, experiment, and play around—Create little tests on anything and everything, without being too disruptive. Test what happens after you alter the sequence of events, reword customer emails, allow a junior employee more responsibility, or print your invoices on colored paper (so they become more visible and get paid faster).

Use visualization—Visualize how changes would happen, what would need to be involved, and where things could change. Albert Einstein spent hours during the day staring out the window and visualizing physics experiments. Similarly, visualizing the details of new ideas can be a great way to try them out before taking action.

Think away from the box—The best ideas and tweaks often come outside of your typical environment. Get out of your office or

---

[4] http://www.forbes.com/sites/matthewherper/2012/02/10/the-truly-staggering-cost-of-inventing-new-drugs/

away from your desk to trigger new thinking. Physical activity such as walking also stimulates the brain for new thoughts on old topics. Even stepping away to get a drink of water or visit the bathroom can trigger an epiphany.

Create prototypes and examples—Prototypes allow you to test ideas before they become a reality. Physical products can get made at a 3-D printer or mocked up by an engineering student or industrial studio. For service products, prototypes can be as simple as a single printed brochure with the new service detailed on it, complete with pricing.

Putting it into Action

Look for areas in the business that are chewing through a lot of costs and see if there are ways to reduce those costs by doing things in a new way. If everyone in the industry has their own in-house art department and you have followed suit, debate whether hiring freelancers or outsourcing might bring in the same quality at a lower cost. Look at your major business practices as if you were an alien from outer space; what would you think of them? What would you think as a young child, a competitor, or yourself 20 years from now? Sometimes, taking the perspective of an outsider can highlight areas that are inefficient, don't make sense, or could be simplified.

Get a small notebook and carry it around with you. As you get thoughts and ideas, jot them down for later. Open up your mind to new ideas by trying different experiences such as art museums, concerts, performances, lectures, talks, readings, new podcasts, and music that you've never heard before. Go for walks, and take extra-long showers. Set the alarm for 15 minutes before you have to wake up and spend the extra time lying in bed, staring at the ceiling, and thinking about solutions to problems. Just after waking up is a great time for creative thinking, so be ready to write down thoughts. All of these methods can stimulate great new ideas.

As you engage in the hard work of thinking creatively, focus on specific experiments, solutions, prototypes, processes, and drawings. This makes it easier to try out your ideas on other people, such as your employees, or perhaps design artists or creative people who will help you.

Project Selection and Management

In Flashpoint 100, you manage a tinderbox (portfolio) of ongoing projects. Some will succeed and some will fail, but overall, the tinderbox will help you reach your goals. A portfolio of projects is better than one big project because not every project makes it, nor should they. The only thing you know for sure is that the unexpected will happen.

Having a tinderbox of projects targeting different benefits and objectives allows you to better weather the problems that come your way. Timelines slip, people underestimate the effort required to get tasks done, employees lose motivation, projects overrun on cost, and things happen that are out of your control. Some projects will get knocked out of the tinderbox when they are tested with customers, while others may get knocked out once suppliers offer pricing quotes. By having a tinderbox, it's more likely that you will have many other projects to push forward when something falls through.

Even large companies make mistakes when they put all of their eggs into one basket. In the 1980s, Coca-Cola spent millions developing, launching, and marketing New Coke. In addition, they pulled the old Coke out of distribution so that consumers would have only one option. This was a spectacular failure—customers hated New Coke. They complained, boycotted the company, and created such a PR disaster that Coca-Cola brought back the old recipe. Surprisingly, Coca-Cola had gone to considerable lengths to test the New Coke product with consumers, and only launched it when they were satisfied it would be a big success. This is the kind of failure you can avoid by managing a tinderbox of projects instead of making just one big bet.[5]

Throughout the process, remember to look at the tinderbox of projects as a portfolio to accomplish the overall goals of the company. This way, even if projects fail, your business goals are reached.

Secrets of Great Project Selection

Great project selection relies on a mix of experimentation and monitoring.
- The funnel approach
- Prototyping and testing
- Setting milestones
- Resource allocation in line with milestones
- Risk-taking
- Tolerance for failure

The funnel approach—Start more projects than you think you will finish. Flashpoint 100 is designed to start big and finish smaller, so only very worthy projects get through the process. Delay or cancel projects that don't reach their milestones or don't have potential. At each Checkpoint, review projects for cancellation and resource allocation. Be ruthless; each project takes time and resources, so don't give any project extra chances if it doesn't deserve it. Do not pursue a project that doesn't have a promising future simply because you've already spent money on it. Money spent is money spent, and you can't get it back.

---

[5] http://www.coca-colacompany.com/history/the-real-story-of-new-coke

Scenario:

At each Checkpoint review, a number of projects are cancelled because they don't hit their milestones. After starting with 25 projects in the beginning, by the end there are 8 projects. However, these last projects have shown potential to bring in additional revenue and solve real issues.

The funnel approach for projects

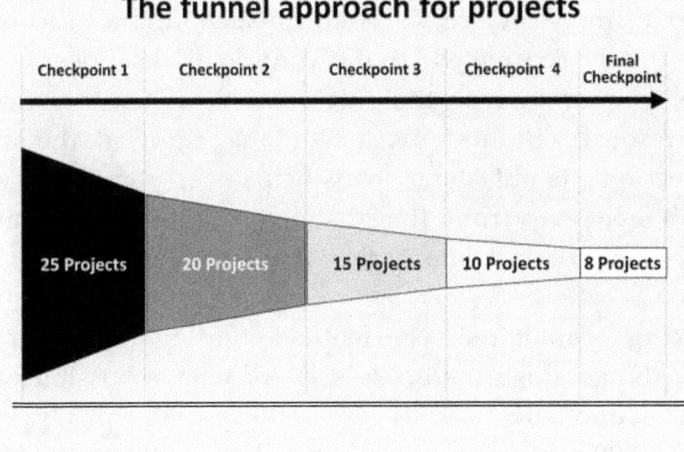

Prototyping and testing — Find ways to break the project down into components that can be tested. This might mean a limited run of a new product, a prototype or mock-up, or another miniature version of the full idea. Then they can be tested in a small part of the business or with a small set of representative customers. This allows you to test the idea before putting the company's full resources behind it.

Setting milestones — Milestones let you compare what *is* happening to what is *supposed* to happen. Good milestones are clear, simple, specific, and include a date. Each should allow the reviewer to tick a simple yes or no without much discussion.

- Bad Example: "Talk to marketing agencies about executing a marketing plan."
- Good Example: "Get three quotes from marketing agencies on a two-month media campaign by June 1."

Make sure the milestone dates line up to completing the project on time.

Resource allocation in line with milestones—Release the money (and other assets) for a project little by little, as projects earn it. For example, in a home renovation project you might put down the money in installments: a third as a deposit to get the work started, a third once the structure has been finished, and a third once the work is finally completed. If the contractor disappears halfway through, you don't lose the full amount. When possible, give projects resources in this way: some money up-front, then more as the project hits its milestones. This helps keep you from spending too much money up-front. It also allows you to initially start more projects, then pull back later if they don't work well.

Risk-taking—Taking risks is essential to finding new opportunities. Try new things. Push the boundaries of what's possible. Ask for things you don't deserve. Try something that will never work. Flashpoint 100 minimizes some of the damage that experimenting causes a company, so now is the time to take risks and attempt the impossible.

Tolerance for failure—Many things won't work out. Don't be concerned when projects don't work, because Flashpoint 100 allows for some projects to fail. Time, money, and effort will be spent on projects that ultimately fail, and this is normal. Only by trying the impossible do you discover what is truly possible. Keep in mind that project failures are not personal failures; employees should not be made responsible for project failures if they pursued success in good faith.

Putting it into Action

As you brainstorm and decide on various projects, try to build a tinderbox that is balanced across a number of different factors.
- Size of impact—large vs. small
- Cost—inexpensive vs. more costly

- Type of impact—revenue-generating vs. cost-saving
- Seniority of project champions (leaders)—junior vs. senior employees
- Difficulty level—easy vs. difficult
- Impact timing—immediate vs. longer term
- Key functions—all functions in the company
- Level of effort—large vs. minimal

It's not necessary to perfectly balance the tinderbox along each of these lines. Just make sure it doesn't become too lopsided with any one area or function taking on the lion's share of the responsibility. For Flashpoint 100 to work, it needs to be a whole-company effort.

Assigning Resources to Projects

Resources (money, time, and assets) are the lifeblood of a company. How much cash you have in the bank determines how much inventory you can purchase and when you can pay employees. Similarly, assigning resources such as cash and employee time to projects is an art that requires careful thought. Ask yourself: what is the best investment? What will be the best return? What is the safest bet? What are the non-financial benefits? Whenever resources are limited, be careful and deliberate about how to use them.

In finance and investment, *capital allocation* refers to how financial resources are assigned to give the best return. To assess the return of a project, finance people look at three main areas: money, time, and risk.

Money—Like the old adage "buy low and sell high," a good investment is one that offers a bigger return than its cost.

Time—A dollar today is worth more than a dollar next year. Even though it's the same amount, getting money earlier is better so you have more time to invest it, spend it, or earn interest on it. This is even more important for small businesses that rely on timely cash flow in order to continue operations. Getting cash as early as possible can make the difference between making payroll and missing it. The amount of money that is 'tied up' because you have to pay employees or suppliers before receiving customer payments is called *working capital,* and it refers to the extra money you need to cover your obligations. For financial investments, there are two time-related components: when the investment is made, and when the benefits are returned. The ideal investment is one in which costs are paid as late as possible, and benefits are received as early as possible. However, many projects require you to pay costs up-front and wait for the benefits to come later. For instance, the benefits of running an advertising campaign will only be seen once the money has been spent, the ad has run, and customers seek out your product and buy it. In this case, it could be weeks or months before the benefits to the investment are seen. The mismatch in time between investment and benefits is unavoidable. However, sometimes it's possible to better match the costs and benefits. This is discussed in more detail in Chapter 13.

Risk—the likelihood of getting the benefits you expect is almost as important as what an investment should return. In the world of finance, risk is so important that it's treated like a cost. High-risk investments are considered more "expensive" than low-risk investments, and investors expect bigger payouts in return. This compensates the investor for taking such a big gamble. For example, when a small company borrows money, it has a much higher interest rate than a large company that borrows. The higher rate makes the loan attractive to lenders who worry about the small company's ability to repay the loan.

For every investment, consider the risk involved so you can assess whether the investment is worth it. The more guaranteed the benefits, the more you should be willing to pay for them. For instance, you'd want to spend more money to get 100 new customers if you were advertising in the same magazine you always use, rather than trying a new one for the first time.

Sometimes, you will make major investments that yield benefits only in the very distant future. While this can be the mark of a company making good decisions, it's still important to be very clear about the return you expect from these investments. These investments should match the long-term vision for the company, helping protect it from competition, irrelevance, or failure. Such investments might include professional development and training programs for new employees that take years to pay off. In this case, the benefit would be a future set of well-trained and highly professional employees.

Ultimately, the aim of Flashpoint 100 is to be as efficient as possible with your money and other resources, so you don't waste them unnecessarily. Some waste is unavoidable, but minimize it as much as possible by holding back on a full investment until you are confident of what the benefits will be.

Secrets of Great Resource Allocation

Great resource allocation links costs to benefits to prevent waste.
- Matching costs to benefits in size
- Matching costs to benefits in time
- Matching costs to benefits in risk
- Measuring out resources

Matching cost to benefits in size—Make sure the investments are "worth it." While there may not be a precise measurement for this benchmark, most managers agree that big investments should return big results. Of course, spending a small amount to get a big benefit is also a good decision. But be wary of any option that involves investing a lot of money while only getting a little back in return. This is not a good investment, because the money would probably be better spent on projects that give a larger return or more surefire results. It's ideal to either match investments to benefits in relative size, or find investments with a very large return on the investment.

Matching costs to benefits in time—Try to delay costs or investments while front-loading benefits as much as possible. This way, your money or other benefits get returned soon after you have invested, which helps to show the effectiveness of the project. It also minimizes the time you spend waiting for the benefits to come in. If the benefits are financial, the faster they get returned, the faster you can do something with that money.

Matching costs to benefits in risk—Factor in the level of certainty for the benefits. Usually, if the investment is something that you've done before, the benefits are more certain and less risky. This could include requesting that production employees work overtime on a popular product that is in short supply.

Sometimes, you might be trying something new without having any idea about what will come out of it, such as sponsoring a local sporting event for the first time. In this case, the benefits are less guaranteed. While these types of new investments are not bad, you can factor this into your investment and planning by giving a bit less money the first time, or do trial runs to see whether or not it works.

Measuring out resources—Allocate resources little by little as milestones are reached in Flashpoint 100. Minimize up-front payments and make them just a portion of the total cost. For instance, instead of giving an approval for a full media advertising campaign, give initial approval for a newspaper ad campaign and tack on advertising for magazines and digital advertising later, depending on how well things go. That way, if the new advertising campaign is not going well, you can pull it and make changes if necessary, without spending all of your money up-front. Do this even if it means giving up bundled discounts—it's not savings if it doesn't work.

Putting it into Action

Measuring out costs and matching them to benefits (in size, time, or risk) takes creativity. It might require special negotiations, calling in favors, or breaking things down into smaller parts. For some suppliers, you might arrange a pay-for-performance model, where you pay according to the benefit you get. In digital advertising, you might pay according to the number of clicks on your website through their advertisement. Other suppliers may be happy to negotiate a payment model based on some money up-front, with the rest given later.

Another option is to break the project down into smaller pieces that can be implemented independently. For example, a major promotional campaign for a new soda might involve supermarket sampling, sampling at a sporting event, and new promotional materials. If you first do the supermarket sampling at one store and get feedback before expanding to more stores or a sporting event, this experience will help you make sure the money is being spent effectively.

Negotiating with suppliers, breaking the project into smaller pieces, experimenting on a smaller scale, and doing things in phases are all ways to break down costs to better guarantee that benefits will be returned.

Motivating Employees

Motivating employees is a critical piece of Flashpoint 100. Many companies think of motivation as a way to get employees to do more work, but in fact it's a benefit for employees, since motivated employees feel a higher sense of satisfaction. Highly motivated employees are a great asset to the company because they are more likely to find problems to fix and challenges to tackle. Highly engaged and motivated employees will want to stay at your company longer and will feel more fulfilled at work. In addition, while financial rewards are welcome, they're not the primary driver for employees. In short, motivated employees are cost-effective, as well as more valuable.

Engaged employees are good for business and essential to Flashpoint 100. Develop different choices, methods, and incentives to work best with people in your company. Some like tangible rewards, while others respond better to positive feedback. Focusing on motivation is not unethical—most employees want to be motivated and challenged. Much of what constitutes good motivation is also just good business. Providing a long list of things to do without the context or big picture can be confusing and demotivating to hardworking staff. While some employees need little encouragement to take on new responsibilities, others only function well when they have a lot of support and accountability from their manager.

Secrets of Motivating Employees

Motivating employees and keeping them engaged requires being transparent and giving ownership.

- The big picture
- Clarity
- Ownership
- Accountability
- Recognition and reward

The big picture—Providing context is important for employees to understand why something needs to be done and how their actions fit in with the bigger picture. For instance, if the intern is assigned the task of updating the sales contact information on the website, he may not understand its importance unless he's told about a new online advertising project to drive customer traffic to the website. With this information, he's able to connect a small task to the goal of increasing sales by 10 percent in the year. This is more likely to motivate him, and he may even have some ideas on how to display contact information or how to upload biographies of the salespeople listed.

Clarity—Clear requirements for employees are absolutely essential to motivate them. It may not be necessary to spell out the exact steps of how to do something, but it's important to make sure the employees understand the expectations and the end goal. When employees are confused, they lose motivation. Worse, they sometimes lose respect for management and are less likely to believe that management knows how to run the process. Being clear helps avoid these issues. Also, increasing clarity on goals helps employees make trade-offs where necessary. Ensure a shared understanding by double checking what people understood from a conversation.

Ownership—Make sure everyone can be in control of something, even if it's just a small part of the process or a single action. Avoid a situation where a small group of people are responsible for the whole Flashpoint 100 process. In addition, ownership helps people get instant feedback on their actions and behavior, while managers can identify the employees who need additional support and those who are doing really well. For instance, actions and projects that are team-led often mean that the strongest or most motivated person takes the lead, while others follow their direction. Someone who contributes a small part toward the project may feel that their work is not recognized or appreciated unless they are named as a contributor to the project in some way.

Accountability—Accountability and ownership are similar, but not identical. Accountability takes ownership one step further, so the person who is the owner has to answer for what is happening on their task. For instance, a project to hire two new salespeople may require that the HR assistant post the job descriptions on an online job board. In the monitoring meetings, address the person accountable for the action directly and ask for status updates. This both motivates them and allows the project champion to understand the type of progress being made on the project. Most employees like having clear accountabilities and roles, and appreciate the opportunity to get credit for something they've done. Assigning a task to a group doesn't ensure that it gets done nearly as well as assigning several tasks to several different people.

Recognition and reward—While financial rewards are always welcome, many people are better motivated by recognition for a job well done, a special contribution, or a particular skill or capability they brought to some part of their work. As a manager, this is good news because it means that money doesn't limit you in recognizing employees for their contributions. To make this especially effective, do the recognition in the middle of the process instead of at the end, so it can serve as additional fuel to keep employees working toward the goal line.

Putting it into Action

The first step in motivating employees is to understand the type of employees you are dealing with. People who are intrinsically motivated are often driven to get things done, tend to be very ambitious, and are very task-oriented. They often like to do things their own way, and may naturally take on a high level of ownership of projects. With these employees, try to give them ownership of projects and action steps that are at their level of capability or even beyond, and give them greater freedom to accomplish what they need to do. Allow them to make decisions on how things will get done, and invite feedback on better ways to do things. Often, these employees are your best assets for growing your company.

Identifying them often comes during the brainstorming process of Flashpoint 100; these employees are the ones with the greatest number of ideas and who are the most engaged. They might also be the most cynical, but also the most willing to give detailed feedback on areas of danger and risk that need to be managed. Convincing these types of employees that they really do have the freedom and responsibility they crave will go a long way to ensuring that projects are done as well as possible.

In contrast, extrinsically motivated people respond better to external motivators: prizes, rewards, or threats of punishment, such as a negative review or feedback. They prefer to have clear goals and rewards to focus on to stay motivated and work towards. In particular, these employees may not say something in advance if a problem is looming on the horizon. Regular meetings (described below) are essential to uncovering where issues are and what needs to be fixed.

Where Not to Compromise

Great endeavors begin with a great plan, and a great plan involves everyone knowing their role and what they are trying to achieve. This book will outline what's needed, step by step, to achieve results in a cost-effective way. While the results will vary by company, nothing will get accomplished if you don't do the work. Overall, Flashpoint 100 is a plan to find major new opportunities and resolve big issues, all while transforming your business in 100 days.

There are other considerations to keep in mind as the plan progresses. How do you keep employees motivated? How do you make decisions on projects? Who should be involved in the review process? How do you ensure that goals are met? How do you know whether you're on track? The detailed description below will address these important questions and others.

The beauty of having objectives and priorities is that when things don't go according to plan, you can easily change course and come up with a new strategy that stays consistent with the overall goal. The only thing you can plan with certainty is that things will not go according to plan. So relax, don't try to predict the future, and keep your eye on the ball. This book gives a detailed method for managing Flashpoint 100, but feel free to make adjustments, personalize it, make it more feasible, or scale it up or down to your capability.

However, while doing Flashpoint 100, there are some areas in which you should not compromise.

- *Timing*—The 100-day period of Flashpoint 100 has been chosen for a reason; that's about how long people can work very hard before getting burned out. It might seem like a short period of time, but the book contains suggestions on ways to extend Flashpoint 100 for some projects when they deserve it. In addition, some projects are designed to be long-term "Game-Changers," so it doesn't mean that all activity ceases after Flashpoint 100 ends. But for the program to work, there has to be a full commitment to completing the program in 100 days.

- *Working toward the super-objective*—Once you start doing things that don't help you achieve the super-objective, then you are in danger. It's a slippery slope from doing something because it seems like a nice idea, to sinking money and effort into an unrelated set of activities. Many employees report that lack of a focused strategy is their company's biggest problem, and this frustration can make the most valuable employees leave. Maintain focus on the super-objective at all times, with one exception: "Housekeeping" projects may not link directly to the super-objective, given that they often address general areas such as professionalism or communication.

- *Trial and error*—Flashpoint 100 is structured so that you get the most out of the time, including experimenting with a number of things to see what is right. Only with a full commitment to a trial-and-error approach will you expand beyond what you think is possible and get early feedback while managing resources in a responsible way. This allows for happy accidents, and helps prevent expensive disasters.

03 ❖ 80

PART 2

GATHER YOUR KINDLING

*Just because something doesn't do what
you planned it to doesn't mean it's useless*

— Thomas Edison

Chapter 4
Vision, Mission, and Values

W hat do you want your company to be in one year, three years, five years, or ten years? What types of products will you have? How many customers will you have? All of these questions are part of the identity and ambitions of the company. Like a child thinking about what she wants to be when she grows up, these ambitions frame how the company sees its choices and what it wants to do. When these ambitions are outlined on paper, it is called the Vision Statement. Furthering this idea, the Mission Statement provides guiding principles for how to get to the vision. Lastly, the Company Values outline the culture that will get you there.

The Vision Statement

The Vision Statement is a short, one-sentence description of your company's ambition or identity. Perhaps your vision is to be #1 in your category, or to be sustainable and with growing profits. The Vision Statement reflects the excellence and ambition of your business. Many well-known global companies have developed Vision Statements following this pattern:

- **Amazon** — "Our vision is to be earth's most customer-centric company; to build a place where people can come to find and discover anything they might want to buy online."[6]

- **Starbucks** — "To share great coffee with our friends and help make the world a little better."[7]

- **Hilton Hotels** — "To fill the earth with the light and warmth of hospitality."[8]

In these cases, the Vision Statements are very "aspirational" — they paint a picture of how good the company will be, without going into a lot of detail. Starbucks even wants to make the world better, through coffee! Good Vision Statements are inspirational and aspirational, helping to motivate employees to achieve the type of world you want to live in.

The Mission Statement

Mission Statements go into more detail about how the vision will be achieved, and include goals or areas where the company will strive for excellence. Mission Statements often spell out which business lines they will target. A good Mission Statement also hints at what the company won't do, which is important for stakeholders

---

[6] http://www.forbes.com/sites/patrickhull/2012/12/19/be-visionary-think-big/

[7] http://www.starbucks.com/about-us/our-heritage

[8] http://www.hiltonworldwide.com/about/mission/

(employees, customers, etc.) to understand where the business will make trade-offs.

Examples of Mission Statements from well-known companies:

- **adidas Group**– "The adidas Group strives to be the global leader in the sporting goods industry with brands built on a passion for sports and a sporting lifestyle. We are committed to continuously strengthening our brands and products to improve our competitive position."[9]

- **BMW Group**—"The BMW Group is the world's leading provider of premium products and premium services for individual mobility."[10]

- **Hilton Hotels**—"To be the preeminent global hospitality company—the first choice of guests, team members, and owners alike."[11]

In these Mission Statements, the companies highlight the focus of the business. In BMW's case, it's "individual mobility," suggesting they won't go into buses or airplanes. adidas Group is clear that they are a sporting goods company and nothing else. See the Vision and Mission Statements, Company Values, and Objectives template in the back of the book for ways to build these.

Company Values

Values are another area where your company can make a difference. As a small set of things your company believes in, values can serve as an important compass for how employees interact and behave, and where the company will not compromise. It also helps to communicate what you want the company culture to be, and

---

[9] http://careers.adidas-group.com/mission-and-values.aspx

[10] http://www.bmwgroup.com/e/0_0_www_bmwgroup_com/unternehme n/unternehmensprofil/strategie/strategie.html

[11] http://www.hiltonworldwide.com/about/mission/

streamlines the hiring process by focusing on only those who hold the same values you do. Core values can relate to a commitment to fairness, transparency, creativity, inspiration, or anything else that links to the vision.

Chapter 5
The Super-Objective and Junior Objectives

O bjectives, goals, and targets are all words for metrics that can be observed, tracked, and monitored. A small number of these can keep you on track by providing an objective assessment of how well you are doing and what you have accomplished. Great metrics are easy to check and difficult to manipulate; they tell the truth, the whole truth, and nothing but the truth. Great metrics are also easy to capture and understand.

What are the Super-Objective and Junior Objectives?

Metrics come in different shapes and sizes. For Flashpoint 100, the objectives are the highest order of metrics. These are the big goals the whole company wants to achieve, and are shared across departments and functions. Accomplishing all the objectives should mean accomplishing the entire goal of Flashpoint 100.

The Super-Objective

The super-objective is the most important metric of the entire process of Flashpoint 100. It functions like the North Star—a guiding reference and set of coordinates that set the path for the whole ship. It's the ultimate priority for the company in the next few months or years until it is accomplished. The super-objective is also important because Flashpoint 100 will rely on a high number of projects to achieve the aims of the company. For this to work, things must point in the same direction.

It's also important that the super-objective is specific and quantitative (numerical). This is because it will be broken down into smaller pieces for different projects, and projects that deliver profit will be measured against it. Some great super-objectives might be "double revenues to $1,000,000 in 2 years," or "hit the 5,000-customer mark," or "increase exports to 50 percent of total production, while growing domestic sales at 5 percent or more." Super-objectives are goals whose meaning everyone can agree on. Good super-objectives rarely use words that have ambiguous meanings, like *best* or *greatest*. Instead, they focus on things that are easy to measure: revenues, profit, customers, number of products, etc. Ideally, the super-objective is something you can measure quickly and easily without the help of an outside agency. This often means not choosing metrics related to brand, competitors, or customer attitudes, because that requires external information such as expensive market audits or surveys.

Junior Objectives

Underneath the super-objective sit junior objectives, which are goals that are smaller, less ambitious, and narrower in scope. Achieving all of the junior objectives should be consistent with achieving the super-objective. Junior objectives help you clarify what you want to achieve, and what you're willing to do to achieve it. Having neither too few nor too many will keep them easy to manage while still achieving the main purpose of Flashpoint 100. Unlike the super-objective, junior objectives can be either quantitative or qualitative:

- **Quantitative junior objectives** are numerical, and easy to measure and monitor. Good quantitative objectives track or measure progress toward a goal, such as number of units sold, quarterly revenue growth, or profit. Make it clear how they link to the super-objective. For example, if a super-objective was "double profit in one year," junior objectives might be related to the number of customers, the amount of revenues, or the number of products sold.

- **Qualitative junior objectives** don't contain numbers and are more descriptive. Often, qualitative junior objectives are used for processes or parts of the business that are difficult to measure. They could include areas such as employee or customer satisfaction, efficiency, communication, collaboration, performance management, fairness, and integrity. Make them as specific as possible so people can "know it when they see it." The litmus test for qualitative objectives is whether five people would agree on an assessment if they were familiar with the situation.

Scenario:
Your training services company made $250,000 in revenue last year. Because you think there are significant opportunities to grow, you decide to choose a goal of $500,000 in revenue for this year. This is your super-objective.

As junior objectives, you decide to choose:
1. Sign an additional six corporate contracts
2. Develop five new training seminars
3. Open a new training center with a partner

Successfully achieving these goals, as well as growing the current customer base, should result in achieving at least $500,000 in revenue next year.

CR ❖ ßO

Chapter 6
Your Starting Point

F inding good objectives begins with understanding your business's current situation. Turning an honest eye to the company helps uncover the issues that are creating drag on your profits, and will also highlight opportunities that can propel the business forward. To get to where the company wants to *be*, it's important to first understand where it *is*. This can be achieved with the help of the <u>Company Diagnostic Template</u> in the Templates section.

It's not necessary to spend too much time on detailed assessments for Flashpoint 100, but it is important to know specific areas of your company's strengths or weaknesses. One to two sentences on each component is sufficient, depending on how complex the issue is.

The first step to understanding your starting point is to take each area in turn and summarize its status. Highlight any major issues or strengths.

Company Diagnostic

The Company Diagnostic gives a snapshot of the whole company, looking at the business from different angles to find its unique strengths and weaknesses. This can be done on your own, but it's good to get other managers, directors, or key employees to review it for input and feedback. Make this an honest assessment of where the company is right now, but don't go into great detail at this stage. Once the key information is gathered, the Company Diagnostic can be done in as little as a few hours.

The Company Diagnostic has three columns: the Area being assessed (e.g., Products), a Description of the area highlighting strengths or weaknesses, and the Level (e.g., number of products offered). Ideally, the level should be a quantitative metric that allows you to measure the difference between before Flashpoint 100 and after.

Financial Performance

A small set of quantitative numbers show your starting baseline performance. These reflect the overall size of the business. These metrics should be quickly and frequently measurable. If your sales system gives you a daily feed of the amount of product that was sold, that's a great place to start.

At a minimum, follow eight metrics related to: volume, revenue, cost of sales, gross margin, fixed costs, cash in the bank, working capital, and earnings, for the last 2 years

- **Financial metrics**

    1. **Volume of units sold**—Depending on your business, this could stand for customers, units, or transactions. Think about what makes the most sense, and what drives the bottom line. If you sell products, choose number of units sold. If you sell subscriptions or bundles of services,

consider measuring customers or average bundle sales. If you are in a "two-sided market," where you facilitate transactions between two parties (like eBay), consider using transactions as this metric.

2. **Revenue (sales)**—This standard number reflects the overall size of the company and is usually easy to measure. For Flashpoint 100, use revenues that are promised to the company, even if they're not paid in yet. For example, if you sell $10,000 worth of product on Day 80 but the customer will only pay on Day 110, you can count this revenue toward your goal.

3. **Cost of sales**—These are the costs to make or perform your actual product or service. Include all of the costs that change, depending on how much you make or perform: raw materials, manufacturing costs, distribution costs, shipping costs, sales commissions, etc. Don't include marketing costs, and don't include things that you have to pay regardless of how much you sell, such as electricity, salaries, or rent. For restaurants, cost of sales would include the food, but not the salaries of the wait staff. For many service-based businesses, the cost of sales may be very low, such as travel expenses and printing of meeting materials. If you do not know how much your product or service costs, find out now.

4. **Gross margin ($ and %)**—Gross margin (amount) is the difference between a product's price and its cost. For instance, if you sell a widget for $3.00 but you bought it for $2.00, then your gross margin is $1.00 ($3.00 minus $2.00). To get the percentage divide the margin amount by the price, e.g. $1.00/$3.00 = 33%. Gross margin directly affects your overall profitability, so it's often a good metric to monitor. If your pricing changes, if you offer significant discounts, or if you have different products or services that are priced differently and cost different amounts, your gross margin will be affected.

5. **Fixed costs**—Fixed costs are the costs that don't change regardless of how much you sell. These usually include overheads like rent, salaries, etc. Sometimes these costs are "lumpy" and are paid all at once; for instance, a license fee. To come up with a monthly total fixed cost figure, add up all your yearly expenses and divide by twelve. For a quarterly figure, do the same but divide by four.

6. **Working capital** —The amount of money that is 'tied up' because you have to pay employees or suppliers before receiving customer payments. Working capital is important because it's the extra money you need to cover your obligations. For instance, if you need to pay suppliers $50,000 for a special order on May 1, but the customer will only pay on July 1, the working capital for this order is $50,000. To find working capital, calculate the extra money needed to make all your required payments before your customers are expected to pay, for a given period (e.g. 4 months).

7. **Cash in the bank**—Cash is different from revenues, because it measures what has actually been spent and what has actually been received, not just what is promised. This is important because the faster you get paid by your clients, and the better terms you have from your suppliers, the more cash you have in the bank. With more cash, you can do more projects, or simply manage the business better (e.g., pay employees earlier or get bulk purchase discounts). Monitoring cash is a valuable metric, especially if some of your customers are not good at paying on time or if suppliers require early payment.

8. **Earnings**—Earnings (profit) before taxes or interest on loans is a great way to measure the overall profitability of the business. The formula to calculate earnings is total revenues minus total costs. For the purposes of Flashpoint 100, don't include one-off costs that are

associated with Flashpoint 100 itself. These are project costs, and will be calculated separately. You may be spending on unusual things that won't normally reflect the business, such as experiments. However, include recurring expenses like annual license fees.

To calculate the amount of cash that is available for Flashpoint 100, the basic formula looks like this:

> (cash in bank) + (3-4x monthly profit after expenses) − (3-4 months' working capital) = TOTAL MONEY AVAILABLE FOR FLASHPOINT 100

- **Business Model**—The types of customers (consumers, businesses), whether you sell direct to end users or via distributors or resellers, and the way you charge them (monthly subscription, one-off pricing, etc.).

- **Marketplace**—Key suppliers, buyers (for business-to-business). If you are in a heavily regulated market, you include your market restrictions.

- **Competition**—The fierceness of the competition and the number of competitors. How are they competing (e.g., on price), and where is there room for you to do more?

- **Products**—The main products and services that you provide, as well as any "star" features or lines that are underperforming, and product prices. If there are a lot of products and prices, list the biggest ones.

- **Marketing**—The main marketing methods that you use, and how well they perform.

- **Target customers**—Your main customers by attitude or motivation, location, or demographics.

- **Gaining and retaining customers**—How you get new customers (e.g., incentives for new members or referrals), and any retention or loyalty programs.

- **Sales and Distribution**—The basic sales model, whether automated or a sales force. Include methods and materials used for sales and account management. For Distribution, summarize the distribution model, such as insourced or outsourced.

- **Company**—Size and shape of the company, including number of offices/sites, their location, and rough number of employees in each.

- **Employees**—The number of people who work for you, their functions, and whether you use consultants/contractors or part-time workers.

- **Operations**—How the operations of the company are structured, and how well-defined or automated the processes are. This includes outsourced processes and the manufacturing or production processes.

- **Partners**—Third parties that help the company survive. They might be distributors, outsourcers, marketing partnerships, affiliates, or companies with bilateral agreements in place.

- **Technology and assets**—Trademarks, patents, logos, and licenses that the company has developed or bought, or relies on to function (software, production equipment, vehicles, etc.).

- **Biggest risks**—The biggest potential risks to the company, either internal (e.g., mismanagement or project failure) or external (a lawsuit or a new competitor).

- **Culture**—How people work together and what they value. Company culture is like a personality, with things that work and don't work. Describe cultural strengths or weaknesses. Are people reliable? Entrepreneurial? Are they diligent, creative, collaborative, and/or personally accountable?

Scenario:

Your company sells sports equipment. Through a partnership, every new customer gets offered a discounted annual membership to the local community center. You also offer an Adventure Club program in which customers rack up points based on purchases and use them for discounts. So far, customers aren't taking up the community center offer, but most enroll in the Adventure Club and make enough purchases to cash in at least one discount. For the Company Diagnostic, this goes under "Gaining and Retaining Customers." You enter it as below:

Gaining and Retaining Customers: Gaining—Discounted annual membership to community center, but it's not really working. Retaining—Adventure Club, and it's very popular.

Scenario:

You run a small accounting software company, selling all-in-one solutions to other small businesses. The company was founded three years ago and you've been growing quickly. You want to consider creating sales or HR software for larger businesses as well. First, you work through a diagnostic of the business to understand where you are today, so that in 100 days' time you can compare.

Company Diagnostic		
Area	**Description**	**Current Level** *(last year)*
Baseline performance	Overall, sales have been strong in the last year. There are 250 total customers, most in the all-in-one package.	−Total units sold: 400 −Revenues: $500k −1-Yr Rev. growth: 20% −Cost of sales: $200k −Gross profit: $300k −Gross profit %: 50% −Fixed costs: $200k −Earnings: $100k

Area	Description	Current Level *(last year)*
		−Cash in bank: $50k −W'king capital: $20k −Total for Flashpoint 100: $20k
Business Model	Via the website and face-to-face sales calls, we sell packages to small business owners, for a subscription.	−N/A
Marketplace	Most other business software companies sell via the website, software, or through other partners. Big companies like Oracle have a number of big packages, but our customers prefer smaller players with better service.	−N/A
Competition	Many companies sell similar software, but just two specialize in the same all-in-one packages: SMESoft and StreamLine. Our customers say we have superior service. Competition is a strength.	−N/A
Products	The main product is the all-in-one package for accounting, marketing, HR, and sales. There is also a resume-management package for recruiting, and a performance-management package for performance reviews. The all-in-one package performs okay, but the HR packages sell really well.	**Prices** −All-in-one pkg: $150/ mo. −HR resume: $20/mo. −HR performance: $20 mo. −HR health costs: $50 mo.
Marketing	We use Google AdWords, some Facebook advertising, and event sponsorships for local Chamber of Commerce events. Digital marketing is more expensive but delivers more customers.	−Monthly spend (avg.): $2k
Target customers	Small business owners with 50 employees or fewer.	−250 monthly subscribers to the all-in-one package
Gaining and Retaining customers	Each new annual subscriber customer gets the first month free ($150 in lost revenue, but not a cost). We also offer a	−Gaining: $150 in foregone revenue −Retaining: none

Area	Description	Current Level *(last year)*
	two-week free trial. No retention incentives. Attrition has grown lately, so this might be a weakness.	
Sales & Distribution	Most sales come through the website, and there are two full-time sales staff selling in face-to-face sales meetings. Sales are paid salaries plus commissions (10% of sales). Website sales are modest at $100,000 annually. Sales staff bring in the majority of business.	−Avg. sales/ salesperson: $200k −Avg. compensation/ salesperson: $100k
Company	One office, headquartered in Seattle, WA. Senior management includes the CEO, CFO, & CTO.	− N/A
Employees	There are 20 employees. Marketing is probably understaffed, and Technology may be overstaffed: two developers spend a lot of time on updates, and it's unclear whether that's necessary. No one is dedicated to business development, special projects, or strategy. This is a weakness.	−20 employees: −CEO −Finance−2 −Marketing−1 −Sales−2 −Cust. support−4 −Technology−7 −Admin office−3
Operations	The Technology team do all product development and updates; the Admin team manages the office, the server space requirements, and licensing contracts.	−1 office −Account with Amazon Web Services (server space)
Partners	One partnership with Prestige Partners, which sells the all-in-one package alongside their own consulting services. They're expensive but good at selling it.	−1 partner− consulting (face-to-face sales) −They take a 20% commission
Technology & Assets	The company owns several patents, which could be licensed to other parties. The name and logo are trademarked in the US. Everything else (office, etc.) is rented.	−3 software patents −Brand trademark (name and logo in USA)
Biggest risks	1. Salespeople aren't able to sell as much (or they leave the company).	−N/A

Area	Description	Current Level *(last year)*
	2. Customers prefer competitors' products. 3. Website continues to underperform.	
Culture	The Technology team is the most powerful; they have the biggest input in product development. Marketing is next in line with decision-making. Sales is expected to sell whatever comes out of Technology. Functions don't work together well, and most employees are engaged but don't take initiative.	–N/A

The Company Diagnostic can take anywhere from one hour to two days to fill out. Go with your gut instinct, and don't spend too much time on precise levels and exact wording. Where there is good data (such as the previous year's total marketing cost) use it. Where there is not (such as the exact size of a competitor) do not try to create it.

PART 3

STRIKE

*The true sign of intelligence is not
knowledge but imagination.*

– Albert Einstein

Chapter 7
Issues, Opportunities, and Ideas

In many companies, everyone agrees what the biggest problems are, but there is rarely time to address them. Little things drag on for months or years without being addressed, just because it's no single person's responsibility to tackle. Maybe it's a pile of unsold inventory for a discontinued product collecting dust in the warehouse, or fixing a small monthly overcharge on a supplier's invoice. Also, there is rarely the time or incentive to address the issues. With Flashpoint 100, now these issues can become front and center. By gathering the team together to openly and honestly put issues on the table, these problems can finally get addressed.

Similarly, longstanding opportunities can be addressed that previously no one has had the time or motivation to explore. This could include things like discovering an old customer request to develop a new feature, a software update that needs to be installed, or filing for a business expansion license. Getting at these requires group discussions and 1:1 meetings to identify areas of concern and promise.

Developing the list of issues, opportunities, and potential solutions is done mainly in brainstorming sessions. As people discuss issues and opportunities, they will naturally begin to offer possible solution areas. Bring a copy of the Company Diagnostic with you, so you can begin ticking off areas of concern that you identified previously. In each meeting, clarify what the issues and opportunities are, then get a list of potential ideas to address them. Make sure the ideas tie to issues or opportunities.

After the full list of specific issues and opportunities is generated, it's then shortened to include only those areas within the company's power to change, particularly in the short-term. These are usually issues related to how it does business, the internal culture and processes, and the products and services it puts into the market. Exclude things outside the company's control, such as the strength of a competitor or the result of a new regulation.

Getting People to Be Honest

Getting good input requires getting people to be honest. Sometimes employees are embarrassed to point out issues in their function or within their team, then these issues go unresolved for a long time. The trick to addressing this is to create an atmosphere that promotes openness, honesty, and anonymity where needed. As much as possible, make the conversation casual. For instance, instead of asking people to document and send in issues, consider conducting the discussion in a roundtable format and include other topics that are less sensitive. Invite people to raise areas of concern, and the rest of the company for input. Ideally, raise issues that face the company as a whole, not just a particular function. For instance, an issue phrased as "low customer retention rates" may cut across the different functions of Sales, Account Management, Product Development, and Marketing. If an issue is phrased as "customers don't come back because Sales misrepresents what we offer," it creates defensiveness. At this early stage, it's important to highlight big company-wide issues, not point fingers at specific individual or departmental failings.

Communication by you as the company head is important. Early on, set expectations for what the company wants to achieve, and how everything will be a team effort. Emphasize that the focus is getting results, not placing blame or highlighting failures. Explain this before any discussions are conducted so that when people arrive for the discussion they are prepared. If the conversation veers toward the blame game, shut it down by redirecting people to concrete issues and action steps.

Another tactic is to collect information outside of open group discussions. Some people may be more comfortable discussing issues in private one-on-one meetings, submitting them in writing, or sending them in anonymously. Make every effort to bring issues and opportunities to the forefront, and don't allow people to keep quiet because they are afraid of upsetting you or others.

Lastly, keep discussions as factual as possible. Request examples of specific scenarios and instances, and look for data or information wherever possible. Avoid letting discussions center on personality or philosophical differences, but instead look for specific events and their effect on the business. Most issues have very complex causes, even if it's down to a single individual who behaves in a particular way. Like a detective, try to get to the root of the problem and don't just accept surface explanations.

One way to understand the root cause of something is to do the 5 Whys technique. Toyota pioneered this process to find problems in its car manufacturing process[12]. For a problem that's been identified, ask the team why it happened. For that answer, ask why again. Do

---

[12] https://hbr.org/2010/04/the-five-whys-for-startups/

this for five iterations in total so you can get to the root cause of a problem.

> **Scenario:**
> Early in the first session, most employees were quiet. Few brought up any issues of significance. Finally, the General Manager (GM) asked about the biggest failure of the previous year. Everyone agreed it was stockouts of the new product shortly before Christmas, which triggered angry phone calls from retailers, a revenue shortfall, then a product surplus in January and February that had to be discounted. By doing the 5 Whys technique, GM learned that the root cause was inadequate notice to Production. Communication was therefore highlighted as a key issue to address going forward.

Setting the Scene

Consider conducting the group discussions off-site, or in an area of the company known for more relaxed discussions (such as the cafeteria or a favorite lunch spot), or the meeting room or office of an advisor or director. This helps take people out of "work mode," making them more comfortable and relaxed so they can speak freely.

Bring large paper (easel paper) and large markers or crayons to capture thoughts in an informal way. You can break people into teams to capture and present issues and opportunities, or have a big brainstorming session with the GM or facilitator writing down the big-picture items that are raised.

Food is a great way to get people to loosen up, open up, and enjoy themselves. People will do *a lot* for a free lunch, especially if it's a nice one. A working lunch where employees are treated to food may help them feel more relaxed and open. Otherwise, snacks and beverages such as fruit, cake, candy, and coffee/tea can stimulate the blood flow and get people talking. Mention in advance that food will be provided; it can be a powerful incentive for people to arrive eager and on time.

Ensure that everyone has an opportunity to speak and provide input. Some people are naturally shy, introverted, or simply unwilling to compete with the loud voices of others. To make sure you capture their input, include a mix of individual written responses and a suggestion box for people to contribute their thoughts. This way, less-talkative people are not forced to compete with more-talkative people to be heard.

In advertising agencies, the team assigned to a big client will have a dedicated meeting room where they meet and brainstorm, keep their materials, and decorate the walls with ideas and planning. This is the "war room" and it serves as a reminder of the client, almost a virtual presence of them in the office.

Creating a war room for Flashpoint 100 can have the same effect. It's a dedicated space for meetings, scheduling, notices, brainstorming ideas, and planning. Depending on the amount of space available, it can be either a full meeting room or even just a corner setup of two chairs and a desk, away from the noise and bustle of the rest of the office. It's important to have some kind of physical space so people can be visually reminded of Flashpoint 100, and also a place where they can go for information (e.g., the number of ongoing projects, or timelines).

Sources of Project Ideas

As issues and opportunities are identified, begin collecting ideas on how these can be addressed. To develop a long list of projects for selection, it's a good idea to start with a very wide range to ensure that a diverse set of viewpoints are included, and that you can be as creative as possible. Everyone's voice should be heard, not just the voices of senior managers. In particular, anyone who deals directly with customers should provide input, because they have special knowledge of what customers want and where the market is moving.

Brainstorming

A good first step is to have a brainstorming session, either as a whole company or within functions. In these brainstorming sessions, get as many ideas as possible from people on how to solve issues and address opportunities. Let people's imaginations run wild, but make sure that each submission addresses a real need. Make sure that quieter voices are also heard. Some people are not as comfortable shouting answers into a loud room, so don't let those with the loudest voices dictate the direction for everyone.

Design firm IDEO is known for their fresh, innovative, and collaborative approach to getting great ideas. They've also created brainstorming guidelines so everyone can get better results[13].

---

7 Rules for Brainstorming
From design and innovation firm IDEO

1. Defer judgment
Creative spaces don't judge. They let the ideas flow so that people can build on each other and foster great ideas. You never know where a good idea is going to come from; the key is to make everyone feel like they can say the idea on their mind and allow others to build on it.

This still means we pose questions and provocations so the ideas can get to a better place.

2. Encourage wild ideas
Wild ideas can often give rise to creative leaps. In thinking about ideas that are wacky or out there, we tend to think about what we

---

[13] https://openideo.com/blog/seven-tips-on-better-brainstorming

really want without the constraints of technology or materials. We can then take those magical possibilities and perhaps invent new technologies to deliver them.

We say embrace the most out-of-the-box notions and *build, build, build...*

3. Build on the ideas of others
Being positive and building on the ideas of others takes some skill. In conversation, we try to use *and* instead of *but...*

4. Stay focused on the topic
We try to keep the discussion on target, otherwise you can diverge beyond the scope of what we're trying to design for.

5. One conversation at a time
Of course...there are lots of conversations happening at once, which is great! Always think about the challenge topic and how this could apply.

6. Be visual
Nothing gets an idea across faster than drawing it. Doesn't matter how terrible of a sketcher you are! It's all about the idea behind your sketch.

7. Go for quantity
Aim for as many new ideas as possible. In a good session, up to 100 ideas are generated in 60 minutes. Crank the ideas out quickly.

By following these guidelines, you can get a lot of good ideas on the table in a very short period of time. Record all recommendations, but don't make any decisions yet on which ones to tackle. However, make sure they are all projects the company can execute on its own with limited outside help. If the projects rely on changes in laws, politics, regulation, climate, or other things beyond the company's control, don't include them.

Suggestion Box

Submissions can and should come from other sources apart from internal brainstorming sessions. Allow people to submit ideas remotely or anonymously, via slips of paper or email. This helps make sure you capture input from all sides. Consider placing a suggestion box stocked with notecards and preprinted forms in a common area. Post signs announcing the reason for the suggestion box, and give guidelines on how to fill out the forms. Print forms requesting a description of the idea, what it would achieve, how it could be done, and how long it would take. Also include a line on the forms for the employee to volunteer for the execution team. Otherwise, they can submit the forms anonymously if they are concerned about how their idea will be received.

Team Members/Stakeholders

Every good effort requires a team. Gathering the right team members and giving them roles or positions to play ensures that you reach the goal with a lot of support along the way. Stakeholders are not just employees, they also include others who have a connection to the company: advisors, board directors, customers, suppliers, and partners.

Advisors and Directors

Advisors and non-executive (independent) board directors can be a source of rich feedback and input. Since they have an obligation to the company, this obligation can be called upon in this time of need. Depending on the level and complexity of the issues to work on, one-on-one meetings with advisors and directors can be ideal. With advisors, this is the time to grill them on the specifics of the company, its weaknesses and strengths, as well as getting ideas of possible solutions and a commitment for support (e.g., that they will find and introduce you to suppliers of cheaper products). Ask advisors to take a holistic view of the company and potential improvements, within the realm of the advisor's expertise. Get a sense of their vision for the company and what it would take to achieve this vision. For instance, if you have an operations advisor, find out the key areas that could drive operational efficiency, the strong or weak processes in your company, and possible benefits and cost requirements for automating manual processes.

Non-executive directors (NEDs) are board members who are not on the management team. Often they are industry experts or former managers of other companies. NEDs should be intimately familiar with the workings of the company. This makes them very useful for several reasons. First, you can draw on their management expertise in other contexts to see where the company can strengthen its business. Perhaps they worked for larger versions of a similar company, or they have started a similar company in the past. This qualifies them to share challenges they have faced and how these challenges were overcome.

Board directors from investors may be able to share other portfolio companies' similar situations and issues, and how they were overcome. Investors are sometimes very useful for brainstorming ideas in areas related to procurement, operational efficiency, managing expenses, collecting payments, contracts, leases, and bank financing.

Customers

Customers are an excellent source of feedback on where the company should focus. Naturally, most of them would highlight "lower cost" as a preferred way to give them greater value. However, by asking more questions about how your service fits into their life or business, you'll gain a much greater understanding of how customers feel about the company.

If your customers are consumers (you are a business-to-consumer company), you will want to know more about the problem your company solves in your customers' lives, and whether you could do it any better. You might realize that you are over-delivering on features or services that customers don't value. If so, these can be scaled back or stopped altogether. Reaching these customers can be done via the usual methods of marketing, on social networks, or at promotional events. Using surveys, focus groups, or simply in-store interviews, you can get their perspectives. This will help you understand what the company is doing well, what to focus on or fix, and which future offerings customers would like to see. Try to get a good cross-section of customers (age, geography, ethnicity, marital status) to reflect many different viewpoints.

How you ask questions of consumers is important. Many people are unable to tell you exactly why they like or dislike something, or whether they would purchase it in the future. Don't rely on these types of questions. Instead, focus on asking them what they value *most* about your product, and have them rank features or identify some that could be eliminated to bring down costs. Also, test them on additional features that can be added, and understand the additional amount that customers would be willing to pay for these features.

You can also use your customers to understand which of your competitors they are using, and why. Are your competitors cheaper, faster, more widely available, or more convenient? Find out now to understand how to win more customers.

If you are a business-to-business (B2B) company, a single customer might be a large, complex organization with many different decision-makers. Making a sale might require the approval of several people, such as department heads, IT, Procurement, and the end user. Each of these people will have specific needs and wants, so getting customer feedback requires speaking to more people. However, you may have a closer and more in-depth relationship to them via your Sales and Account Management teams, so leverage them to get access in the right way.

If you have a face-to-face sales model, work with your sales functions to schedule a meeting with each of your top customers. Conduct the meeting in an informal way, but make sure that you end the meeting understanding your role with them, what you are doing well, why they continue to buy from you, how to get them to buy from you in the future, and any changes they would like to see. Lastly, ask what else you should do. These meetings can be very effective over lunch, which is a good incentive for them to give you their valuable time.

If you do not have a face-to-face sales model, calling customers and requesting phone or face-to-face interviews with them can get you the required information, and is often much appreciated. Position it as an honest request for feedback, and make sure to thank them for their business. To get a range of perspectives, talk to both your frequent customers (super-customers) and occasional customers. Super-customers are loyal, long-term, and often exclusive users of your company. They prefer you to your competitors, and usually drive your bottom line. They are very familiar with your business and can give you constructive feedback. Occasional customers won't know your business as well, but they can give you a good comparison of your company against your competitors, and a good assessment of things you can do to get more of their business.

Suppliers

Most companies have good relationships with their suppliers, but rarely ask them for input or advice on their business. They should, because suppliers can be great sources of opportunities and suggestions for improvement. As experts in their fields, many welcome the opportunity to have an honest conversation about how your company can improve. Although suppliers' primary concern is making money, you can still ask what to do to lower costs. Suppliers can be a great resource to understand how you can be more efficient, save money, or get more value from the services you already buy. Have a frank conversation about how to qualify for discounts, and what else they can do for you.

Your suppliers may also do business with your competitors, so there's an opportunity to know about how you stack up against the competition. While they probably won't give you secrets about the competition, they may be able to say where the averages are and how you compare. For instance, suppliers can give you a sense of how you compare in terms of efficiency, ordering, usage, buying, quantities, ranges of products, customization, etc.

Partners and Third Parties

Distribution partners, third parties, licensors, and other partners can also be great sources of feedback and resources for ideas of new ways to do things. Since they are already in business with you, it's in their best interest to help you grow your business. They may be able to give tips on best practices based on their business or their other partners. They may even be able to sign new deals, offer barter deals, or include favorable terms for new partnerships.

Chapter 8
Project Selection

DAY 8

Building the Tinderbox

Building your tinderbox of Flashpoint 100 projects is probably the single most important thing you will do. The good news is that it should come easily from the work you've done to identify issues, opportunities, and ideas. At this point, it's best to come up with as many ideas and potential solutions as possible. Later on, you can select which projects to start.

To begin, pretend that the company has an infinite number of people and an infinite amount of cash. What would you do? As a manager, develop as long a list as possible, but make sure that each action/initiative:

- addresses either a problem or opportunity discovered in the Issues and Opportunities sessions, or,
- helps achieve at least one of the objectives or gets you closer to the company's vision

Addressing a problem or opportunity area is important because it's easy to get in the habit of doing things for their own sake, without thinking how it fits into the big picture. When you are a small business, there are many things you can do, but trying to do them all at once with no underlying plan risks pulling the company in too many directions simultaneously. Each project will be evaluated by how well it actually fixes a problem or allows you to target an opportunity area. By making this criteria clear from the beginning, it's easier to later tie it to specific benefits.

Scenario:

The supplier of an important input has prices that vary by as much as 20 percent from month to month, based on a fluctuating market rate. This makes it difficult to predict your profitability on a monthly basis, and sometimes has forced you to take a bank loan to make payroll, which is undesirable and expensive. To address this, you develop a project called Long-Term Contract for Input X. This project involves negotiating a long-term contract for a fixed price with the supplier, where you commit to a minimum monthly order for the next six months in exchange for a fixed-price guarantee slightly above the average price for the year. This directly fixes the problem of pricing variability.

Most of the projects should be aimed at addressing opportunities. These ideas can come from many different areas: underserved segments of customers, failing competitors, a technology that allows you to do new activities in a low-cost way, a new supplier input that you can sell to customers, or simply a new idea you've discovered.

Scenario:

There might be an opportunity to insource graphic design for your creative agency. Recently, a southern European country that is strong in design talent began experiencing economic difficulties and as a result, many top designers are out of work. You can now hire and bring over talented designers at an affordable price, building an in-house design team that wows customers.

Scenario:

As a food company, retail store distribution is a major issue, and you don't have enough distribution trucks to satisfy growing customer demand. There are regular stockouts, and loyal customers are forced to use a competitor's products. Expanding the fleet of distribution trucks would be costly and time-consuming to buy and paint the trucks, then hire and train drivers. Recently, the problem was discussed in a board meeting with investors, who are also investors in a big beverage company with a large fleet of distribution trucks serving the same stores as you. Once the investors learned of the problem, they suggested that you strike a deal with the beverage company to distribute your products. This would give you instant access to a fleet large enough to satisfy demand, and the beverage company would benefit from additional revenue with minimal additional costs. The investors offer to make the introductions and encourage the deal.

Creating an Initial List of Ideas

Go/No-Go Areas

While you talk to employees, stakeholders, and other sources for ideas, begin noting rules and principles that guide what you do and what you won't do. Every company should have a set of rules they live by, that they will not violate for the sake of short-term profit.

Similarly, every company will have a set of things that are an easy yes if it comes up, because it's so well-matched with what the business wants to do that there's no need to debate. These are the Go/No-Go areas.

Go areas are in line with the company's vision and mission. They match what your ambition is and how you plan on getting there.

No-Go areas are the opposite; they are areas you won't go into because they don't match your vision, mission, or values. They are the off-limits areas that make you uncomfortable, are unethical, or simply don't match who you want to be. For a luxury brand, this might be selling at a discount. For a food company, it might be producing cosmetics. Begin developing a list of 5 to 10 No-Go areas that you and your top employees can agree are not things you'll do in the near future. This will make it easier to make decisions later.

Scenario:
You run three high-end sandwich cafes in a small college town. After talking to your customers, you realize that what people love most about you are the gourmet ingredients, which you source from local farmers in the area. You realize this something special that you don't want to give up. You record the following as Go and No-Go areas:

Go areas
- Gourmet extensions
- Distribution extensions (e.g., grocery)
- Other types of high-end cafes, restaurants, and bars
- Partnerships with companies that have the same vision

No-Go areas
- Mass production
- Low- quality ingredients
- Franchising in areas with no local produce
- Non-food production

Getting to the First Cut

Once you've received all the submissions, it's time to get to the first cut, or initial list. If you've done your sourcing, discussions, brainstorming, and submissions well, you now have a long list of potential ideas and projects to consider. Some may seem like such good ideas that you are ready to run out and start doing them immediately. But not so fast!

All ideas need to go through a quick two-stage filter in order to decide which ones get discarded and which ones get built out for further consideration. The stages are:

- *Feasibility filter*—Discard the ideas that are not feasible, would take too much time to change or implement (like 10 years), or are outside the company's control (such as changing a law).
- *Go/No-Go filter*—Filter the list through your Go/No-Go areas. Discard anything that doesn't fit the list.

Once this is done, don't bother prioritizing further. Right now it's important to get the longer list and begin thinking about how to get enough information to decide whether to do them or not. In the next section, we'll discuss how to get the information you need to make a good decision.

Chapter 9
Project Champions and Project Teams

DAY 8

Building the Team: Finding Project Champions (Owners)

Each initiative, no matter how small, needs a champion who will be the cheerleader for the initiative. The project champion ultimately is the person of record for the project. The project champion also acts as the project manager, ensuring that milestones happen within budget and on time. This is important because a single person needs to be fully accountable for requirements, negotiating for resources and others' time, and handling discussions on how the initiative is progressing. The project champion may not be doing all of the work, but they should be able to guide how the work is done and oversee the process. Having a single project champion ensures that the ball doesn't get dropped between people involved, and gives a clear line of accountability.

To maximize engagement and spread the work, find project champions across the company from junior to senior levels. Junior employees make great project champions for smaller projects, such as Housekeeping and

Low-Hanging Fruit (discussed in more detail in the next chapter). This helps to empower junior people and also ensure that senior people are freed to focus on larger projects. Junior employees can be monitored by managers, but they should be considered in charge of the project. This gives them a chance to shine, to own something, and also to show their ability to take action and manage something. Their line managers should continue to support them, however. Ultimately, the function head is responsible for ensuring that projects within his or her function are done to standard and on time. If a junior employee is not up to the task of managing a project, he or she can be redirected to another team and someone else can serve as the project champion.

Senior people are a good fit to oversee more challenging or complex projects, particularly the Meat and Potatoes and Game-Changers ones (discussed in more detail in the next chapter). Meat and Potatoes projects can often be done within a particular function. An example might be a major marketing promotion, overseen by the Marketing function head. Game-Changers, however, often require significant support across many functions. Game-Changers, such as launching a new product, may require the support of Marketing, Sales, Finance, and Operations. However, a single project champion should oversee the completion of the project and manage the contributions of the function heads. This person will probably be a senior person in the company, such as head of Sales, but they may choose to work closely with one of their direct reports to do the day-to-day coordination.

Although senior people will be project champions, they may not be doing most of the work themselves. Later chapters will address delegation and action owners. At a minimum, the project champion should be able to collect data on progress, understand problem areas, and be confident that the project is being managed to the best of his department's abilities.

Creating the Supporting Team

Once project champions have been selected, teams can be created for the larger projects. This team answers to the project champion, and ultimately helps deliver the initiative. For example, a marketing push may elect the function head as the project champion, but another two or three people on the project team will make the phone calls, work with marketing and design agencies, and monitor social media. All team members will report to the project champion regardless of the typical reporting lines. This could mean that someone more senior reports to someone more junior for a project.

Choose teams based on the barest minimum requirement to successfully push the project forward, and balance them for diversity, contributions, and capability. Ideally, larger teams will have a cross-section of members from different functions. For instance, a project to outsource a production process might include members from Operations, Product Management, and Finance. Employees can be on several projects at once, though the sum total should not exceed what they can deliver at any given time. This balance can be achieved by focusing on the timing of their contributions during Flashpoint 100. For instance, a Finance employee may need to give early input into the configuration of a new enterprise resource planning (ERP) system, but very late input into a new logo design. If there are key people who need to input into many teams, consider scheduling the projects around those people. Remember, do everything possible to remove obstacles and free up time to pursue the projects.

Team members' time can be further freed by considering temporary help and support during Flashpoint 100. For instance, temporary administrative employees, a lawyer on retainer, a professional copywriter, or a PR firm on retainer could free up your employees.

Chapter 10
The Four Types of Projects

B ecause Flashpoint 100 is designed to deliver immediate as well as long-term growth, a balanced mix of projects gives the right blend of opportunities. Balancing projects also helps spread the effort and reward across employees and functions.

There are four types of Flashpoint 100 projects, varying in complexity, time required to implement, and the ultimate payoff. Your final set of projects should span the four buckets of Game-Changers, Meat and Potatoes, Low-Hanging Fruit, and Housekeeping.

Game-Changer Projects

Game-Changers are the most complex projects in Flashpoint 100, but deliver the biggest rewards. They are big, they are audacious, and they will cause major change in the company. Game-Changers often require many people to work on them, along with significant costs and other resources. However, they are usually worth it. No project is too big to be considered, so think big and audacious. Later in the book, we will explore how to take it forward cost-effectively and quickly, and how to know whether it's working so you can drop it in favor of something else. But for now, put everything on the table for consideration and give it an honest effort.

During the 100 days of Flashpoint 100, the purpose of Game-Changers is to get a very good understanding of whether to do the project and what the outcome would be, based on solid market validation and thorough feasibility analysis. This may sound simple, but it still requires a lot of work. By the end of the period, Game-Changers will be identified, assessed, scoped, tested, and prepared for a decision meeting on whether or not to take them forward.

Examples of Game-Changers

- Expanding operations into a new market
- Adding new products or services
- Insourcing or outsourcing major activities
- Changing your business model in a significant way
- Acquiring or merging with another company
- Forming a joint venture
- Opening a new office, store, or production facility
- Launching a new brand
- Relocating the company or changing the headquarters

Types of Game-Changers

While a Game-Changer is any project that takes significant effort to deliver (more than 100 days) and has a major impact on the bottom line, many different types of projects can fit into this category.

- **Top-line Game-Changers** deliver a sales or revenue uplift, or major expansion in the business. Many of these are very large projects that fundamentally change the nature of the company or what it can do. This category includes anything that would increase revenue significantly, such as mergers/acquisitions, major capability improvements, new products or services, and geographic expansions. Some examples for this category include buying a competitor, developing a new product, establishing a new co-branding partnership, or developing a joint venture.

- **Bottom-line Game-Changers** impact cost, efficiency, or profitability. Often these are ways to be more efficient, better at managing a costly part of the business, more sustainable in the long-term, or more cost-efficient. Some options might include a new distribution partnership, insourcing or outsourcing plans, a factory or office consolidation plan, purchasing a supplier, or redesigning a factory.

- **Organizational Game-Changers** don't necessarily affect either the top line or the bottom line right away, but might prepare the company for growth or create value in the long-term. These projects often relate to the location or structure of the offices or facilities, performance management and reporting lines of employees, or culture change. Examples of organizational Game-Changers could include reorganizing the company, changing reporting lines, creating a new department, relocating a factory, moving the headquarters, centralizing operations in one market, or creating a new office.

Choosing the Number of Game-Changers during Flashpoint 100

Remember, the goal for Game-Changers in Flashpoint 100 is to do enough research and vetting for a decision at the end of the period. To make the decision in 100 days, it's important to choose several Game-Changers that can be evaluated at once. Instead of picking one possible new product, choose several. For a relocation, evaluate different possible relocation sites, and choose different reorganization options. At the end of the 100 days, decision-makers will be able to confidently decide on the ones to choose, the reason why these are the best, and what the impact will be.

Testing

As much as possible, identify ways for Game-Changer projects to be tested before they are fully implemented. For instance, if you are a food company, conduct tests and samples within the company of a new product then test-market with a small group of potential customers before going into full production. Small-batch food production whipped up in your kitchen and served to friends and relatives alongside Yes/No cards can be a money-saving way to identify new foods to enter the bigger testing process.

Getting a small group of target customers from your friends, network, and the public can serve as a ready-made focus group for testing new consumer-facing ideas. A lot of time can also be saved by recruiting 20 to 100 people and paying them to appear in the office at regular intervals to give feedback on new packages, products, and marketing. Other options include regular trips down to the mall or local coffee shops to ask people about their opinion on new potential products.

Since the goal of testing Game-Changer projects is to understand whether they will work if they are fully launched, try to identify success criteria early on. Like a scientist conducting a high-level experiment, choose criteria that will prove or disprove the Game-Changer as the right project to back, and hold yourself to this. If you reach 20 people in your target customer segment and no one likes the new product idea, change something: the target customers, the idea, or the way it's being communicated. The goal is to get as much inexpensive feedback as early as possible to prevent mistakes, or at least reduce their frequency.

Meat and Potatoes Projects

Unlike Game-Changers, Meat and Potatoes projects can be executed within 100 days, and the benefits are felt immediately. However, they may be complex to deliver and require cross-functional support from the company. They also show just how much you can get done in a short period of time. Benefits from Meat and Potatoes projects are long-lasting and can contribute in a major way to the top or bottom line. Choose Meat and Potatoes projects based on their ability to be completed within 100 days, their ability to deliver lasting results, and their cost/benefit profile.

Examples of Meat and Potatoes Projects

- **Partnerships**—creating new partnerships with agencies, distributors, suppliers, or complementary service providers.
- **Marketing surges**—marketing initiatives that update the brand, new campaigns across different types of media, customer testing and research.
- **Product/service offer changes**—new pricing plans, bundled offers, or new payment plans.
- **Distribution and sales**—new salespeople, new campaigns, enhanced customer management, new customer relationship software, a new distribution model, or a new distribution channel.
- **New promotional items**—testing new packaging, one-off discounts, free gifts, or bulk offers.
- **Competitive intelligence**—Mystery shopping of the competition, taste tests of your product vs. the competition, or surveys of customer attitudes toward the competition.
- **Conferences and events**—private events where you can invite current and prospective customers, speaking or exhibiting at industry conferences, or delivering training programs.
- **Organizational development changes**—promoting worthy people, reorganizing the company to enhance information flow or efficiency, creating new positions in the company,

major hiring in a function, training and development plans, office or store renovations, collocating key employees, or creating new HR policies to reward high performers.

- **Back office**—implementing new systems in payroll, accounting, or inventory management, or creating a new customer credit policy.

Remember, while the major work of Meat and Potatoes projects will be completed in 100 days, there may be more resources required to support them on an ongoing basis, such as customer service support, sales staff, warehouse space, etc.

Low-Hanging Fruit Projects

Low-Hanging Fruit refers to the juicy, accessible projects that don't take much effort to implement and have an immediate benefit. These projects can be executed within less than 100 days, with immediate benefits. Many of them will be "no-brainers" that are easy to communicate and relatively easy to execute. In some cases, the Low-Hanging Fruit creates one-off value that's never seen again; in others, lasting change. For the Low-Hanging Fruit, nothing is too small as long as it doesn't drain a lot of resources. Low-Hanging Fruit projects need proper scoping and management, but are typically straightforward. Measure what works and fix what doesn't, but mostly use Flashpoint 100 to spend the effort and watch the results.

Examples of Low-Hanging Fruit Projects

- **Marketing**—Updating marketing materials and messages to reflect any new products or services, issuing a discount or short-term promotion, creating social media accounts for the first time, collecting client or customer info for an email marketing campaign, calling or visiting customers to sell more, or conducting a customer survey to get feedback.
- **Inventory and product management**—Selling off discontinued inventory, conducting overdue stocktaking,

benchmarking against competitors' product features, discontinuing products that aren't selling.

- **Suppliers**—Reviewing other suppliers to see if they can deliver better quality at similar prices, applying a supplier credit, looking for discounts you qualify for, renegotiating existing pricing based on past loyalty or volume discounts or future commitments.

- **Back office**—Going through accounts receivable to find collectable amounts, changing customer credit terms, applying for payment card loyalty programs, signing up for free trials, renegotiating leasing contracts, or switching banking partners to save money.

One way to understand how to design these projects is to talk to friends, peers, or community members. Find out how the local pizza place improved their pizza delivery times, how the local clothing boutique reduced their excess inventory, or how the local dry cleaner renegotiated their lease. Many of these business owners can be found through your local Chamber of Commerce, breakfast networking meeting, or business association.

Many Low-Hanging Fruit projects require some investigation or research in advance. You may need to know local or national regulations, cost for an email marketing program, or the total amount owed by clients.

Housekeeping Projects

Housekeeping projects can make a big difference over the long run, but their benefits are difficult to measure. These projects are often the unsexy initiatives that get overlooked because they don't directly impact profit or revenues. However, *not* doing them often causes frustration, duplicated processes, and missed opportunities. Overall, Housekeeping projects usually make the company more professional and more sustainable. They can also facilitate other projects, increase employee happiness or productivity, or reduce the risk and threats in the company. The aim of Housekeeping projects could be to improve communication, reduce time on activities (especially admin), reduce errors, improve information management, or improve efficiency. In some cases, the benefits from Housekeeping projects won't be felt for months or years.

To sniff out Housekeeping projects, ask employees and management what would make their lives easier. Listen to common complaints and grumbles, and look for solutions that would improve things. If your employees have heard of specific technologies, programs, or processes that streamline existing ways of doing things, write those down as possible ideas. If not, identify what would make their lives easier. For example, perhaps there is a lot of manual data entry that the Finance team does, or Sales must fill out expenses multiple times in different systems, or function heads lack a forum for exchanging ideas or challenging each other. Build a list of Housekeeping projects that are balanced across ease of execution, cost, time to pull off, and size of future benefit.

Select Housekeeping projects based on their consistency with the kind of company described in your Vision Statement. Could your current systems and processes handle 50 percent more customers, or 100 percent more? If not, now's the time to implement some projects that will help prepare the company for further growth. You are planning for the company of the future, not the present.

Other Housekeeping projects might come from ongoing issues that many people know about but just never quite got around to. This might include updating the website or employee contact information, upgrading office equipment, or reorganizing the office so that team members sit together.

Benefits from Housekeeping projects are usually qualitative and can't be easily measured. They might include streamlined processes, better communication between functions or managers, happier and more productive employees, better data tracking, and better overall monitoring of the company. Rarely can they be tied to a quantitative impact, such as lowering costs or increasing customer numbers. This is why they get their own category, so they won't get overlooked in the frenzy of achieving profitable growth.

Examples of Housekeeping Projects

- **Systems and processes**—Documenting key processes (e.g., procurement approval process), developing contingency plans, upgrading IT equipment, or replacing aging equipment or furniture.
- **Employees**—Implementing a new expense tracking system, designing a training or personal development program, or instituting regular performance reviews.
- **Organizational**—creating a CSR (corporate social responsibility) program, identifying a company charity, reorganizing the company's reporting lines and divisions.
- **Communication and knowledge management**—Instituting 30-minute weekly management meetings, starting a company newsletter, or creating a knowledge management system.
- **Sales and Marketing**—Clearing the backlog of customer requests, updating the website and other marketing materials, or reviewing the Sales commission system.
- **Inventory and product management**—Reviewing and updating certifications, licenses, and permits; or implementing a new inventory management system.

Many Housekeeping projects make a company more competitive and sustainable in the long term.

ଔ❖ଓ

Chapter 11
Building the Project Profile

N ow that you know the _types_ of projects that will make up the tinderbox, it's time to begin identifying and selecting _specific_ projects. The general principle is to identify as many as possible, then whittle them down later based on agreed-upon selection criteria. This keeps good ideas from being dismissed prematurely.

When describing projects, it's important to have enough detail so the meaning is clear to everyone who comes to the project cold. Scope each project fully and give it a clear set of action steps, dates, expected benefits, and expected costs. This is essential for managing the progress of each of the projects, and to ensure that each continues to be worth the effort. See the Project Profile Template in the Templates section to do this.

Developing the Project Profile

Decide what the key objective is	Break the project down into key components	Agree milestones in line with checkpoints	Systematically go after each component
For every project, decide what you want to get out of it	Decide the steps to get the project done, so you can check 'yes/no' when they are completed	Set dates for each action step, and assign a single owner to each action step to make it easier to track	Component by component, go after completing each action step

The Project Profile Components

Each project profile sheet contains the following.

1. Name. Give each project a name that clearly describes what the project does, for example "Marketing Surge" or "Investigate Call Center Outsourcing." If the project is sensitive in nature, it can be given a code name, like "Project London" or "Project Wizard".

2. Code. The Project Code quickly references the project. A good method to use is the first letter of the main function, followed by a number (e.g., M1, M2, M3 for Marketing projects, S1, S2, S3 for Sales projects). This helps in case the project's name or scope changes.

3. Project Champion. The person responsible for overseeing the project, who makes sure it goes forward.

4. Type of Project. Whether the project is a Game-Changer, Meat and Potatoes, Low-Hanging Fruit, or Housekeeping.

5. Summary. A description of the initiative, one to two paragraphs maximum.

6. Junior objectives. Which of the junior objectives this project applies to.

7. Length. How long the project will take, in days.

8. Start date. When the project is due to start.

9. Purpose. What the project will accomplish. This answers the question, why should we bother? Or, what will it get us? The Purpose allows managers and directors to double check the internal logic of the project. They can also examine the underlying assumptions tied to the project's success, and question the benefits that will come from doing the project. For instance, if a project calls for "greater media spend" with the rationale of "increasing brand awareness", managers may ask how much awareness is expected, and whether increased brand awareness is part of the junior objectives.

10. Required information. The pre-work needed to get the initiative started, such as the necessary data, activities, or approvals. For instance, required information for a new CRM (sales management) system might be the needs of the Sales team.

11. Activities, Activity Owner, Completion Dates, and Status. This is the main section of the project profile, outlining exact steps, times, accountabilities, and status levels. Be as detailed as is reasonably possible so that the business and the board (or management) understand exactly what's required and how the initiative is progressing. It's not important to go into a lot of detail, but it is important to give enough information that someone can quickly see whether or not an activity is done. Language is key; using words that are broad or vague can cause confusion. Instead of "talk to software vendors about new point-of-sale system," a better activity description might be "get quotes from three point-of-sale vendors." Remember, each activity line will be checked Yes/No for whether it's been accomplished, so make that evaluation easy. A good example follows.

#	Activity	Activity Owner	Date to be Completed	Current Status
1	Get quotes from 3 promotional agencies	Suzy Q	31 December	Not started

12. Impact. Each function that's impacted should sign off on the projects of other business units to ensure the achievement of proper approvals (e.g., in spending) and notifications (e.g., in production). The purpose is better overall alignment, to avoid bottlenecks and delays. Many companies have functions that primarily drive revenue, such as Product Development and Sales, and functions that support them, such as Finance and Legal. Quite often, the revenue-driving functions create new projects that the support functions must accommodate, but if the flow is not planned properly, then large delays can be the result. For instance, if Sales and Marketing ramp up their efforts at the same time, it could create major demand that catches Production off guard. Suddenly receiving a lot of new orders with no warning is a recipe for both unhappy Production people and disappointed customers.

13. Costs (operational expenditure, capital expenditure). The cost profile is very important, and the tools provided can help you manage it. The total amount shown is the total that the project will need, and when it will be needed. The total should be split into operating expenditure (opex), and capital expenditure (capex).

Opex is the increase in ongoing expenses that the company will see, or costs spent in the normal course of doing business. These are things like salaries, rent, buying inventory, marketing, etc.

Capex is spending on investments in property, equipment, or things that don't happen in the normal course of business but make the business bigger or more valuable. Usually these are one-off costs, such as buying a new machine or vehicle, software upgrades, or new computer equipment. For example, hiring a new employee is an increase in opex, while buying a new laptop for her is an increase in capex.

Also, include whether the required cost is needed all at once, or in installments (e.g., monthly), whether it's fixed or variable, and why. For instance, a marketing survey may increase in cost with the number of customers surveyed. As you outline this, check to make sure that the levels are appropriate, and whether similar results could be achieved with less investment. For instance, are you upgrading to the deluxe package without checking whether it's needed?

14. Benefits. Benefits can be either quantitative or qualitative, and the full set of projects should include a mix of both quantitative and qualitative benefits that are easy to measure, are important to the business, and contribute directly to the bottom line. The best quantitative benefits increase the number of customers, the number of product units or service contracts sold (volume), revenue, or cost savings. Qualitative benefits are harder to measure, but most people in the company should be able to agree that these benefits are needed and beneficial to the company, such as ranking as the favorite among customers, or creating the best product in a particular quality feature.

15. Risks. Risks are little threats or obstacles that could derail the whole project. Highlight these in advance so you can see them coming and make appropriate plans. Risks could be anything from a competitor that launches the new product you are testing, or failing to get the proper permits from the government for expansion plans. Thinking these problems through in advance means that you will be better prepared to face them in the event of a problem. It also allows you to evaluate whether a project failed for a legitimate reason or for lack of effort.

The Importance of Milestones

Each activity is assigned a due date in order to make it a milestone. Milestones are ways to keep projects on track and evaluated for whether they should be stopped, delayed, or given additional resources. Space milestones out so they don't all fall toward the beginning or end of the project. They should also be progressive, with each step building on the previous one.

Scenario:
You run a small bakery in an affluent neighborhood, selling specialty breads and pastries to consumers, restaurants, and health food stores. Your products are upmarket and healthy and cater to people on restricted diets, such as no-sugar and gluten-free. You decide to set up a Meat and Potatoes project to increase sales.

Project Code: **M1**
Project Name: Neighborhood Sampling
Project Champion: Tony, head of Sales
Type of Project: Meat and Potatoes
Length of Project: 60 days
Start date: March 1 (immediately)
Junior Objectives: Double revenues to $200,000, make brand a household name among target customers
Purpose: Raise brand awareness and create consumer demand.
Description: Do extensive sampling via partnerships and in-store sampling to stimulate sales with local residents. At two local health food stores where our goods are sold (Nature's Way and Whole Earth), we will use existing staff to conduct all-day Saturday sampling of products via special stands. In the new vegetarian restaurant Veganopolis, we will offer free gluten-free biscuits as table bread, provided that our company name is prominently displayed on the bread basket. Next month, we will also give away free samples at the local street fair.

Required information, data, and research to begin execution
- Agreement from head baker on extra production requirements
- Any city restrictions on giving out samples at the street fair
- Costs of giving away free product
- Additional sales required to break even on free product giveaways

---

Project Steps

#	Activity	Comple-tion Date	Action owner	Status
1	Sign agreement with manager of Veganopolis on free product for the restaurant—days, products, amounts	March 8	Fred	In progress
2	Sign agreement with manager of Nature's Way on sampling plan—days, products, amounts	March 10	Sarah	Done
3	Sign agreement with manager of Whole Earth on sampling plan—days, products, amounts	March 15	Sarah	Done
4	Develop sampling plan of product, amount, and logistics (delivery times and locations)	March 22	Fred	In progress
5	Design and print cards for Veganopolis bread baskets, store signs for daily sampling, and display baskets for street fair	March 25	Fred	Not started
6	Conduct first delivery of product to Veganopolis	March 30	Fred	Not started
7	Conduct first Saturday sampling at Nature's Way	April 1	Tony	Not started
8	Conduct first Saturday sampling at Whole Earth	April 8	Tony	Not started
9	Conduct street fair sampling plan	April 15	Fred/Tony/Sarah	Not started
10	Measure uptick in revenues in each store	April 22	Fred	Not started

Impact on other functions

#	Function	Predicted impact	Notifications/ Approvals
1	Production	Additional production for sampling	Approval of sampling plan
2	Finance	Additional costs, break-even analysis, revenue measurement	Notification for tracking, approval of sampling plan and for additional ingredients
3	Admin	Additional coordination and logistics support (deliveries by hand)	Notification of required support (days, times, responsibilities)

Required resources

#	Resources	Cost: Capex	Cost: Opex	Date needed	Person responsible
1	Cardstock, signs, display baskets	$0	$200	25 March	Fred
2	Additional supplies for free product	$0	$400	30 March	Fred

Benefits

#	Benefit	Target level	Target date
1	Additional 'Likes' to the Facebook page	200	May 1
2	Increase in sales of product sold in Nature's Way and Whole Earth	Increase in each store during sampling weeks from $100 to $200, for an additional $200 in total from the two stores each week	Starting April 15
3	Increase in sales in the main store due to higher recognition	In-store sales increase 10% from $1,000 to $1,100 weekly, for an additional $100/week	Starting April 29
	Total benefits	$300 weekly for 8 weeks minimum = additional $2,400 in revenues	

Risks

#	Risk	How to mitigate
1	No new customers visiting the store from Veganopolis sampling	Stop Veganopolis promotion after 2-4 weeks, offer coupons to Veganopolis customers who come to the store later on
2	Promotional sampling in Nature's Way and Whole Earth doesn't stimulate more sales	Stop Nature's Way and Whole Earth sampling after 2–4 weeks, redesign stands and train employees where to find product in the store, create special 'today only!' discount promotion

C8 ❖ 80

Chapter 12
Making the Final Cut

Take a deep breath. You've just done a lot of work: you've identified a lot of potential projects, you've thought about how they would work, you've looked at what they would bring you and what they would cost, and you've done some preliminary research. Now, take a step back and see the projects that you want to take forward—any holes in the projects, and the tasks to do first. Creating a tinderbox of projects is an art, not a science, so it's not critical to do it perfectly the first time. Making the final decision on projects should take a maximum of one to two days.

Review

Read through each project's junior objectives, descriptions, activities, timing, and the costs and benefits. Check whether they make sense on their own, and together. Do the costs line up with the benefits? Do the assumptions make sense? Can everything get done in a reasonable amount of time? Are there enough people available? Can you really achieve that amount of growth?

Making Kill-or-Proceed Decisions

Now comes the tough part. There is a good chance that not all projects can proceed as imagined. Some don't stack up to their own logic; they repeat the aims of other projects, they're too risky, or they take too much of a toll on the company. It's better to kill or put off projects now than sink time and resources into a project that will never deliver.

Once the profile is built, it's time to evaluate whether to proceed, re-scope, or cancel the project. The decision depends on the needs of the company, the type of project, and the required time, money, and effort to complete it. You can also make an assessment based on the risk level or the feasibility of the "things that need to go right." For each project profile, make one of three decisions:

- **Proceed.** After looking over the project profile, do a quick cost-benefit check to determine whether it's worth the money, effort, and time, given the benefits it will deliver. If it's a Housekeeping project, few of these will provide big benefits, but they contribute qualitative benefits (professionalism, communication improvements, growth potential, or efficiency). If the reason not to proceed is that you can "do it later," do it now. The purpose of Flashpoint 100 is to get things out of the way so that they don't drift along for long periods of time. Evaluate Low-Hanging Fruit projects based on whether the benefits will be be guaranteed and the effort will be minimal. Review Meat and Potatoes projects for the amount they can deliver within the 100-day period. For Game-Changers, decide whether it's worth going through the effort to do the proper scoping and market testing to make an ultimate decision.

- **Re-scope.** If the project is not ready to be launched, or if it seems to require too much effort, it might need to be re-scoped. Re-scoping involves redefining the actions of the project to make it smaller, or increasing it to deliver more. Re-scoping will require sending it back to the project champion with very clear instructions on the areas to change, and how to scale the project up or down. Explain how changes in one area (e.g., the amount of money invested) might affect changes in another area (e.g., future sales uplift). Also, make it clear whether you want more detail, a smaller version that's more manageable, a bigger version that delivers more results, or a different focus. Be as specific as possible, and offer to work with the project champion if they don't understand what you are asking for.

- **Kill.** If you've reviewed the project profile and decided it's just not worth the effort, kill the project. It's important to make the decision based solely on the merits of the profile, rather than the amount of time already spent on scoping it or the enthusiasm of the project champion. If it doesn't stack up, it doesn't stack up. The projects in the 'kill' bucket may not be lost forever, however, so do not destroy the profiles. Keep them stored in case other projects fall through and need to be replaced, or if circumstances change so that the profiles become more attractive. For example, if certifications for a new food product are too costly to justify a new product release, then you might kill the project. However, if regulations change so that certification is no longer needed, it might be worth developing the new food product. When you kill a project, try to reassign the project champion to another team, even if not in a leadership role. If the project champion already has other projects, this is less of a priority.

Scenario:

The marketing manager has submitted an impressive Meat and Potatoes proposal for new packaging based around an upcoming sporting event in a major city. It requires significant support from Graphics, Production, and Product Management to design the new package and get it to market. The project will take approximately eight weeks and will cost $8,000, but could bring in $10,000 in earnings. After reviewing the effort required, you ask the marketing manager to re-scope the project so that the new package can be used all over the country, not just the city hosting the sporting event. In this way, you can roll it out to more cities, and for a cost of $8,000 you can make $15,000 in earnings.

Scenario:

A major competitor is no longer producing their bulk offering for wholesale distribution. Your sales manager sees this as a great opportunity for you to produce the bulk product, since you can get their old customers without doing much work. Distribution and storage costs will go up, since you will have to rent more warehouse space and also change the distribution schedule of the trucks to deliver on demand instead of the current fixed schedule. After reviewing the risks and the benefits, you decide to kill the project because the new distribution plans will disrupt the existing operations and be a lot of work. More importantly, it's not clear whether the competitor stopped producing the bulk option due to low demand.

Sequencing

Proper project sequencing determines how much gets done by factoring in bottlenecks and balance. A bottleneck is a part of the process that can slow everything down. For instance, if every new customer to your software service must be registered by a Customer Service representative, then Customer Service could be a bottleneck and you need to plan around their availability. If the bottleneck is cash from operations, then sequence projects based on the expected cash in the bank. This might lead you to do the bigger-payoff projects first so you can use the additional cash to finance smaller-payoff projects later. If the bottleneck relates to particular functions, such as the Sales or Finance, then plan based on their capacity. Free up as much of their time as possible, and get them involved early on in the planning of projects so they can offer suggestions on how to be more effective.

At any given time, you will probably want to have a mix of the quick-win projects that are easy to do and get out of the way, plus the more complicated Game-Changer projects. This will help you balance the wins and accomplishments, help morale, and give a feeling of accomplishment.

Timing projects is not an exact science; it's more of a matter of what feels right based on your company's capability and your desired level of accomplishment. Some of these general considerations will help you decide when to start each project.

- Try to prevent a big bump of projects starting all at once, and start some of the smaller projects immediately. The goal is to minimize fatigue and burnout, and help employees start to see immediate results.
- Balance projects across functions to prevent some functions being overloaded while others are idle.
- Begin complex projects earlier, allowing for time to adjust or add more resources as other projects finish.
- Make sure several quick wins are achieved in the beginning. This helps people feel a sense of accomplishment.

Project Tinderbox Analysis

A quick analysis of the project tinderbox will tell you whether you are due to meet your goal, and the benefits to expect for the cost. Tools at the back of the book can help with this process. The analysis phase tells you a few simple things: the amount that it will cost, the amount that will be returned to you, the amount that you need at each point, the people who are doing certain tasks, and the timing of their task completion.

Data to Use for Analysis

The quantitative analysis is based on quick-and-dirty conversions of different metrics into a single overriding metric, usually earnings (profit). For instance, if your gross profit margin (profit on sales before you pay fixed costs) on each unit sold is 30 percent, then every $1 of additional revenue is worth $0.30 in gross profit (30% × $1= $0.30).

For each project designed to increase sales, you can apply your gross profit margin to get the equivalent amount of earnings. For Flashpoint 100, you are encouraged to convert everything to earnings. Then, subtract project costs to get a final profit figure (net profit). In this way, you can separate the ongoing profitability of a project from its up-front costs.

Net Profit Formula: Earnings - Project Costs = Net Profit

Every quantitative metric should be convertible to earnings. To keep things simple, use estimates. For instance, if you had 400 customers last year and total revenues of $200,000, assign a revenue per customer value of $500.

Revenue per Customer Estimate Formula: Total Revenue ($200,000) ÷ Number of Customers (400) = Revenue/Customer ($500)

Other good data points can be converted to a profit metric:

- **Cost savings**: cost savings typically improve earnings by the amount of the savings. If you lower your production costs by $1,000 per year without changing anything else, you will have an additional $1,000 in earnings per year.

- **Revenues**: Revenues are converted based on their percent (%) of gross margin. As in the example above, if you get an average of 30 percent gross margin on each sale, convert revenues to earnings at 30 percent.

- **Price increase**: Price increases, if they don't affect sales numbers or accrue additional costs, directly increase earnings. For example, if you sell bottled juice for $1.50 and each costs $1 to make, your gross profit is $0.50 ($1.50 - $1.00 = $0.50). If you then raise the price to $2, your gross profit is now $1.00 ($2.00 - $1.00 = $1.00). The increase in earnings is the additional gross profit multiplied by the number of bottles you sell.

- **New customers**: New customers are profitable depending on the amount of revenue they bring in, and how much profit you get on that revenue. Use averages, and divide your revenue by the total number of customers to get your revenue per customer. Then, apply your gross margin percentage to that number to understand how much gross profit each new customer generates [(Total Revenues ÷ Total Customers) × Gross Profit %]. For example, if total revenues were $200,000 and total customers were 400, then each customer is worth $500 in revenue ($200,000 ÷ 400 = $500). If your gross profit percentage is 30 percent, then each customer is worth $150 in gross profit ($500 × 30% = $150).

- **New units sold**: Converting new units sold to gross profit is as simple as using the gross margin percentage (30 percent in our example) to the average price of your products. If the price varies hugely, use a weighted average price, multiplying the price of each type of product by the relative proportion of that product in your total sales.

Scenario:
Your company sells two types of vacuum cleaners: handheld vacuum cleaners for $40 and full-size upright vacuum cleaners for $200. Last year you sold 1,000 total units, where 900 (90%) were handheld vacuum cleaners and 100 (10%) were upright vacuum cleaners. Finding an average price is difficult because of the big difference in pricing between the two products. You want to export to a new country and are not sure how to estimate the potential sales, because you are not sure what price to use.

To find the average price, create a weighted average using the proportion of each product and its price:
Handheld
- The proportion of handheld vacuum cleaners is 90%
- The price of handheld vacuum cleaners is $40
- The proportion times price of handheld vacuum cleaners is 90% × $40 = $36. This number represents the contribution of handheld vacuum cleaners to the average price

Upright
- The proportion of upright vacuum cleaners is 10%
- The price of upright vacuum cleaners is $200
- The proportion times price of upright vacuum cleaners is 10% × $200 = $20. This number represents the contribution of upright vacuum cleaners to the average price

Adding the contribution of handheld and upright vacuum cleaners together, you get $36 + $20 = $56. This is your weighted average price.

Use this number as the average price for every project that is not product-specific. When you add the revenues from exporting to a new country, use $56 as the average price for new units.

By using existing data to convert everything to earnings, each metric can be summed up to produce a total for Flashpoint 100. Remember, these are just estimates, not precise numbers. The purpose is to understand the relative impact so you can better compare different initiatives against one another. If you are highly analytical, feel free to add more precision to the numbers. If you are not analytical, it's better to deal with estimates.

Scenario:

You sell a type of smartphone speakers for $50, and it costs you $20 to manufacture them, including materials (but not including overhead like rent and salaries). Your customers love the speakers so much that almost everyone buys one set, then another set a few months later as a gift. Therefore, each new customer represents two sale units.

Right now you make $200,000 in revenue every year, and your total costs are $100,000. You sold 4,000 units last year to 2,000 customers, and you plan to get an additional 1,000 customers this year. You also think you can raise the price by $10 per unit with no loss of sales, because competitors are charging much more for an inferior product. In addition, with the increased volume you can now get a bulk supplier, which will shave $5 off your per-unit cost.

Below is your table of conversion metrics.

In total, your changes look like this:

- Additional customers: 1,000
- Price increase: $10
- Per-unit cost saving: $5

In this case, each major metric is converted to an earnings value, based on projected performance. Note that this does not include project costs (which will be subtracted later). Make sure you do not double count.

Table of Conversion Metrics				
Metric	Description	Explanation of conversion	Conversion formula to Earnings	Values to be converted	Earnings equiv-alent
Earnings %	The proportion of each sale that your company keeps as profit after paying all costs and expenses	Total profit is calculated as a proportion of revenue and expressed as a percentage (%).	(Revenue - Total costs)÷Revenue	($200k-$100k)÷$200k	50%
New customers	Additional customers that you sell to for the first time	Average number of purchases a customer makes in a year, multiplied by the average order size, multiplied by the earnings percentage.	Extra customers × avg. # customer purchases × average order size × earnings %	1,000 × 2 × $50 × 50%	$50k
Unit sold	A single sale of a good or service	The earnings percentage of a single unit sold. If you have many products, use averages.	Unit price × earnings %	N/A	-
Revenue increase	Additional sales, income, or revenue, measured in currency (e.g., US$)	To get earnings, multiply the earnings percentage times the additional revenue.	Earnings % × revenue increase	N/A	-

Table of Conversion Metrics

Metric	Description	Explanation of conversion	Conversion formula to Earnings	Values to be converted	Earnings equivalent
Cost reduction	Reductions in your operating costs, or in the unit cost to produce something	Cost reductions automatically increase the amount of Earnings	– (operating costs) Cost reductions × 100% – (unit costs) Cost reductions × 100% × # of units	(unit costs) $5 × 4,000	$20k
Price increase	Increase in the average price per unit	Price increases (difference between new and old prices) increase Earnings by 100% if no new costs are involved. To get the figure, multiply the price increase by the number of units sold. For many products, use the average price increase.	Price increase × number of units sold	$10 × 6,000	$60k
EARNINGS					*$130k*

Once your metrics have been converted, it's simple to do totals and tallies by the type of project, function, or any other categorization. By comparing functions, you can see which ones contributed the most to the overall earnings, and which ones created the highest amount of costs. Not every project or function will create a positive earnings figure. Remember, since some functions are not customer-facing (such as Finance), it's normal that they would create costs but not revenue. But these functions are critical to support revenue generation, so don't overlook investing in them. For instance, an enterprise resource planning (ERP) software application might make it much easier for Finance to track expenses, inventory, and payments received. It may cost thousands of dollars to implement, but ultimately it will mean lower expenses, more customers paying on time, and fewer of outstanding invoices. This contributes to more net profit (and more cash in the bank).

The Cost Analysis

The cost analysis has two main components: the total cost of all the projects, and the timing of these costs. It's important to know whether payments are due up-front or at the end, because this will impact the amount of cash you have. The ideal schedule allows you to stagger costs and pay them out bit by bit. The cost analysis also shows which projects or functions are responsible for the most costs.

The Benefits Analysis

As discussed earlier, benefits fall into one of two buckets: qualitative or quantitative. Qualitative benefits are non-numerical, but descriptive. Review them and ask yourself the question: do these benefits make us the company we want to be? Quantitative benefits, which are much easier to assess, will probably span several different types of categories: new customers, new revenues, cost reductions, etc. It is also helpful to convert each quantitative benefit into a single metric, such as earnings. For instance, how much gross margin (earnings) do you keep on each dollar made? To calculate the earnings of a new customer, multiply the average number of times they buy from you times the average amount they buy (in dollars), times your gross margin percentage.

Formula: (Average # Times Customers Buy) × (Average Amount Bought in $) × (Profit %) = New Customer Earnings

---

Scenario:

On average, a customer spends $20 whenever they buy flowers from your small florist. Most customers buy twice a year for about five years before they move out of the neighborhood. That means new each customer is worth $200 in revenue total ($20 price × 2x per year × 5 years= $200).

Every $20 bouquet you sell costs you $5 from the floral distributor, so your gross margin is $15 on each bouquet ($20 - $5=$15). Therefore, your gross margin percentage is 75% ($15 ÷ $20=75%). Using this logic and what you know about customers, each new customer is worth $150 in earnings ($200 in customer revenues × 75% gross margin = $150).

The shop manager has submitted a project profile to bring in 30 new customers. With the metrics above, you know this represents about $4,500 in earnings ($150 in new customer earnings × 30 new customers). The project will only cost $200 in postage and printing to execute, so you know it is a good deal.

Scenario:
You have written profiles for all the projects in your tinderbox. Now you will fill out the template in the back of the book to analyze the benefits. Your gross margin is 30 percent, and all cost savings go directly into earnings. You want to know how much the full Flashpoint 100 program will deliver once all projects are finished.

Projects and Benefits by Department (page 1 of 3)					
Department	Project	Benefits	Project costs	1-Year Earnings	1-Year Net Profit
Marketing	M1. Marketing Campaign	Sales campaign- $20,000 in sales			
		Customer Service inquiries +10%	$1,000	$7,000	$6,000
		Increase in brand awareness			
	M2. Retail Audit	Stockouts reduced to 5%	$5,000	$10,000	$5,000
	M3. Brand Research	Knowledge of strengths and weaknesses of brand	N/A	N/A	-
	M4. Develop (P&L) for each Brand	Monitoring	N/A	N/A	-
Sales & Distribution	S1. Distributor incentives	$10,000 savings in 1 year	$2,000	$12,000	$10,000
	S2. Distributor database	$1,000 savings in 1 year	$0	$1,000	$1,000

	Projects and Benefits by Department (page 2 of 3)				
Department	Project	Benefit	Project costs	1-Year Earnings	1-Year Net Profit
	P1. Supplier validation	$25,000 cost saving for the year	$0	$25,000	$25,000
Production	P3. Asset purchases	Cost saving approx. $50,000	$150,000	$200,000	$50,000
	P4. Production Planning Process	Cost saving approx. $30,000	$0	$30,000	$30,000
	F1. Finance processes	Less waste, streamlined activities	$0	N/A	-
Finance	F2. Working capital reduction to manageable levels	Outstanding invoices - Bring from 55 to 30	$0	N/A	-
		Reduce overdraft to $15,000	$0	$200	$200
	F3. Centralized information database	Better knowledge management	N/A	N/A	-

Projects and Benefits by Department (page 3 of 3)					
Department	Project	Benefit	Project costs	1-Year Earnings	1-Year Net Profit
HR	H1. Address labor turnover	Attrition to 5%	N/A	N/A	-
	H2. Long-term motivation plan	Higher employee engagement	N/A	N/A	-
	H3. Employee satisfaction surveys	55% satisfied	N/A	N/A	-
	H4. Employee referral program	Hiring costs reduced to $2,000 from $7,000 per employee	$5,000	$5,000	$25,000
Other	O1. Board calendar, charter	Better board management	N/A	N/A	-
	O2. All-company communication plan	Employees	N/A	N/A	-
TOTAL				$152,200	

Another way to look at impact is to review the functions or people who are sponsoring the highest number of projects. Plotting each of these out in a map or timeline (see Templates in the Appendix) will clearly highlight exactly who is doing what, and can prevent departmental overload.

Example

Number of Projects by Function

	Number of projects	% of total
Finance	4	14%
Marketing	7	25%
Sales	3	11%
HR	2	7%
Production	12	43%
Total	*28*	

Production has 43% of all the projects. This could be a big strain for them

Once you have lined up all the costs and benefits and impact, take a step back and see what you've created. Ask yourself:
- Does it make sense?
- Is it what you expected?
- Does it look too easy?
- Does it look too difficult?

The timeline, list of projects by function, and total costs should add up to be a bit more than what you think you can handle. Since not every project will make it through the process, it's better to start with more than you need. In addition, it's important to force yourself to make decisions between projects when some are underperforming. This helps you justify how you use time and resources. Instead of just rolling along with something for the sake of it, projects will have to justify their existence on a regular basis so that you will not waste a lot of time and resources. It's also easier to be bold and take bigger risks when you can pull the plug on something that isn't working. This allows you to commit to some wild and crazy projects.

Once you have finished doing the analysis, take another look to see what needs to be rearranged. Inevitably, some projects will make more sense at the end versus the beginning, or require a different project champion who will have more time or capacity to take them forward.

Doing the Cost and Profit Analysis on the Tinderbox

Another form of analysis is looking at the cost and profit profile of the tinderbox, to visualize the impact of the costs and benefits on the company. For simplicity, look at the costs and benefits for three periods: the first few months of Flashpoint 100, the first year (including Flashpoint 100), and the first two years (including the first year). Sometimes this method won't capture the benefits of the Game-Changers, but that's okay.

Remember, these are just estimates and projections, not hard and fast numbers. The reality will be nothing like the forecast, but it's important to line up all the expected costs and benefits to see if they make sense today. Don't be alarmed if net profit is negative for the first few months, or even the first year. It's common to invest early on and only see the full benefits much later. Plus, many of the Housekeeping projects may require up-front costs but will not deliver much profit directly.

Example:

In this example, project total costs grows modestly, project earnings increases considerably, and therefore project net profit increases a lot. In the first three months, however, net profit is negative. This is common, since many of the costs of Flashpoint 100 will need to come earlier rather than later.

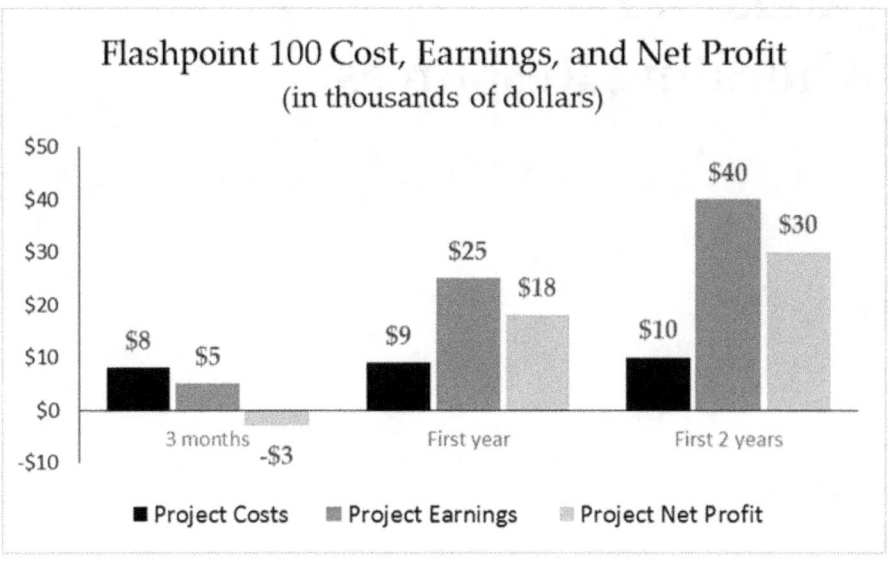

Chapter 13
Allocating Resources

W ith everything that's been done so far, now ask yourself: "how much will all of this cost?" By knowing what's required for Flashpoint 100 and being smart about your spending, you can get the most from your resources.

What are Resources?

Anything that a company owns that has limited access or a finite amount, which the company needs to function, is a resource. For Flashpoint 100 this includes money, inventory, materials, furniture, property, machinery, staff, etc. Resources are important because they are expensive to build up, so you must be careful about how much and how often you use them, to make sure it's worth it. A key principle of Flashpoint 100 is efficient resource management to prevent waste and help prioritize activities.

Types of Resources

Cash

Cash is the most valuable resource your company has. Different from revenue, which is money owed, cash refers to the amount of money on hand. Cash management is critical to any small business, and is based on how quickly you collect payments from customers, how quickly you pay suppliers, when you pay expenses and salaries, and how much cash you get from other sources (investors, partners, etc.). While cash that's owed by customers and promised by investors is nice to think about, it's no match for how much money is actually in the bank. Therefore, in Flashpoint 100, *cash* means funds that are available immediately.

When a company begins the Flashpoint 100 process, it should be very healthy: profitable, regular revenues, and significant cash in the bank. The Flashpoint 100 process is intense and requires having enough money to do the basic experiments and implementation. Cash is not spent needlessly or carelessly, but projects that will drive value need investment. For this reason, it's recommended that the company have significant cash in the bank, or a solid assurance from investors to support Flashpoint 100.

Assets

An asset is any tangible or non-tangible item owned by the company that makes it more valuable, and could potentially be sold. A manufacturing company typically has tangible assets such as factories, machinery, warehouses, and delivery trucks. Assets can also be intangible, such as software, licenses, or patents and trademarks. Like cash, assets are finite and should be planned in tandem with Flashpoint 100. For instance, if one Flashpoint 100 project includes finding new products to test-market, the factory may need to set aside machinery and some equipment to make small test batches. This could affect their regular production schedule.

Support Functions and Internal Specialists

Companies may have functions or key employees that are critically important in the day-to-day running of the company. Often, the purpose of these functions is to ensure the proper functioning of other teams or people. Key employees that fit in this category are often assigned to positions in Sales, Customer Service, HR, Finance/Accounting, Procurement, and Legal. If a project involves hiring 10 new people, this has to be coordinated and supported by HR. Similarly, contracts requiring legal signoff will need to be scheduled and reviewed by Legal employees or contracted firms. Releasing a new promotional item may require Customer Service to add temporary or permanent staff to handle the additional demand.

It's especially important to allow these employees to step back from their day-to-day work in order to support the broader Flashpoint 100 effort. This helps prevent them from becoming bottlenecks. To free up their time, get a good understanding of their current level of work and the amount of their time needed to support projects. Interview them as early as possible to understand the arrangements that can be made to free up their time and allow them to focus on supporting the broader effort.

Partners—Agencies, Outsources, Distributors

Many companies rely on external agencies, consultants, or outsourced firms to do parts of their work: PR agencies, marketing agencies, distributors, call centers, etc. You will probably need to alert them to Flashpoint 100, and let them know that you may have special requests or want to conduct trials and experiments. Many of these types of companies will be delighted to work with you in a new and different way, and may agree to the complimentary use of some of their services, such as social media campaign analytics.

> **Scenario:**
> After a quick review of company assets, you realize that your retainer contract with your PR agency covers any and all PR, not just the product set that you currently have. Instead of increasing the marketing budget for a planned new product, you ask the PR agency to work on getting press for the new promotional product you will temporarily offer.

Other resources

Sometimes small companies have access to special privileges, people, or favors. These can be treated as resources as well, even informal ones like help from the social-media-genius niece of the CEO, time from the web-developing brother of the accountant, favors owed by the marketing person's former supplier, or volunteered freebies from personal friends. During Flashpoint 100, it's important to look at creative ways to get things done, including friends or people in your network who are willing to support the effort. So don't be afraid to reach out to advisors, investors, directors, family members, or friends to see how they can help.

As you allocate resources, add the cost-benefit profile into the decision, which is what you get in return for providing resources to projects. Apart from the totals, it's also a good idea to evaluate the timing of costs and benefits. It also allows you to answer questions like:

- Are these cost levels appropriate?
- Could similar result be achieved with less investment?
- Is the benefit timing good?
- Does the timing justify investment at these levels?

One challenge with many projects is that costs are up-front, while the benefits come later. This makes it difficult to be confident that you are doing the right thing. However, there are some ways to make this less of a challenge.

- **Costs linked to benefits**—If possible, try to make cost payouts in small pieces as benefits trickle in, and minimize the time between when costs are paid and benefits are seen. This allows you to see how well something works before paying out a large amount.

- **Guaranteed benefits**—Pay attention to the certainty of the benefits; a better guarantee increases your confidence in paying out costs up-front. If it is something you've done many times and are confident how it will work out, then there is less risk with an early cost payout. For instance, if you are executing a known advertising campaign for something that always delivers an increase in sales, it's okay to pay everything up-front. However, if you are trying something new, it's better to minimize the up-front costs until you know more about the impact.

- **Low costs/high benefits**—When the benefits are very large in relation to the costs to get them, then it's usually an easy decision to do the project. For example, if a supplier with financial difficulties offers a 20% discount on merchandise in exchange for a cash purchase of next month's inventory, then the additional cost (money taken out of the bank a month earlier) is minimal in comparison to the benefit (20% discount).

Three ways to match costs to benefits
All assume that the benefits are greater than the costs

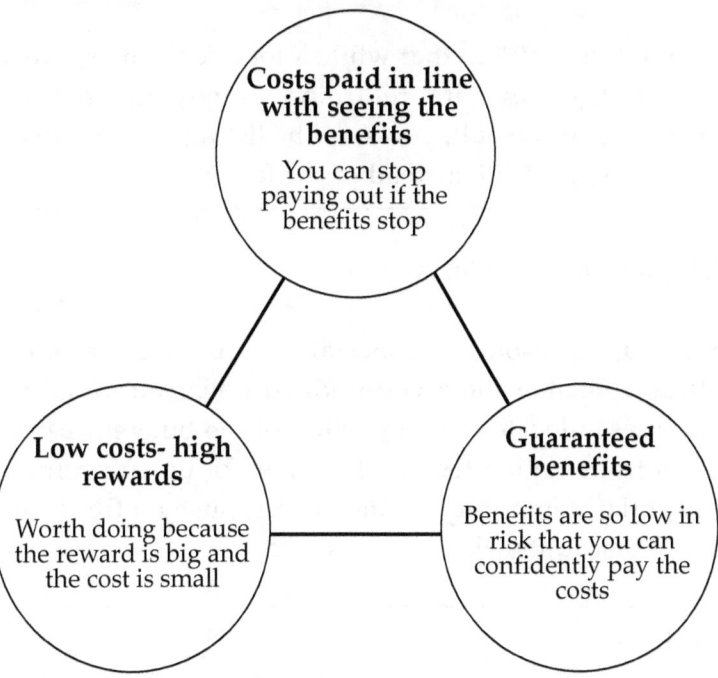

These three ways to match costs to benefits can help you evaluate whether a project is worth doing, and whether it needs to be re-scoped to better match the costs to benefits.

Scenario:

A discount site approaches you about listing your company with them. They've asked you to buy an annual package, which would feature your brand and a regular special offer. Their sales agents have promised that customers typically purchase a discount at 30 percent off, and then return to your business two to three times to purchase additional products or services at full price. It sounds fantastic, but there's no way to be sure that this will happen. The annual listing is $1,000, but since you are not sure, you negotiate paying $150 per month on a month-to-month basis. During that time, you track the customers who come in from the site and whether they buy again.

Because of this, you see that while a lot of customers are buying the initial deal, few are returning to buy the regular-price merchandise. As a result, you stop the listing two months in, and you've only spent $300 instead of the full $1,000.

Allocating Resources in Stages

When allocating resources, especially cash, set out a schedule. In order to stay flexible and account for cost overruns or address new opportunities, allocate only a portion of the budget up-front. This keeps you from paying too much money for unsuccessful projects. Try to negotiate temporary arrangements, push for free trials, or ask for one-off discounts wherever possible.

Scenario:
You have $10,000 to spend new projects. Once you have agreed which projects to implement, you allocate and spend only $2,500, leaving $7,500 to "drip feed" to projects when they meet their goals. After the next Checkpoint in three weeks, most projects are doing well so you pay another $2,500, leaving $5,000 remaining. By the second Checkpoint, only a few projects have survived, so you allocate only $1,000 to those projects, leaving $4,000 remaining. This saved you $4,000, since not all projects were successful. If you had spent the $10,000 in week one, then you would not have saved $4,000.

Chapter 14
Freeing up Employee Time

Finding the time for senior management and employees to put aside their day-to-day responsibilities is one of the biggest challenges of Flashpoint 100. You cannot underestimate the dedication, patience, and contributions from employees to get it done. Doing this will require you to understand what is critical and must continue, and what can be pushed aside for a while. For instance, Customer Service needs to be just as available for customer inquiries, but end-of-the-month reports perhaps can be put on hold. If you can, schedule Flashpoint 100 to happen *after* performance evaluations, so that employees feel freer in taking risks without feeling like it will factor into their performance evaluations.

Set Employees Free!

Ask your employees to free up their time by wrapping up or tying off existing projects, and setting many other processes to autopilot. Give them permission to let some things go for a while, such as some administrative tasks, while they focus on Flashpoint 100.

Find non-essential items that can be suspended or delayed, such as running routine monitoring reports or filing expenses. Consider outsourcing, automating, and hiring agencies or consultants to take up the slack in other areas such as blog posts, marketing plans, monitoring, social media management, etc. Tasks that are administrative in nature may be handled by an outside source. This could free up an extra hour or two per day for employees within a function like Sales or Accounting. Interns can be brought in to handle some of the data tracking, monitoring, and management for the projects themselves.

Set clear expectations on the amount of time employees spend on Flashpoint 100 execution. In general, the more senior the employee, the more time they should spend. Senior-level managers may spend half of their time on Flashpoint 100, while more junior employees may spend most of their time on their regular work.

New work schedules should be drawn up, communicated, and agreed upon, such as scheduled overtime or additional hours for the 100-day period. This isn't easy, because it's asking a lot to tear people away from their main responsibilities, even for short periods of time. However, most motivated employees genuinely want to participate in exciting new changes that could improve the company in the long-term. In short, find a way to make it work that doesn't compromise the core business, but still allows enough employee attention to accomplish new tasks.

> **Scenario:**
> At your office, sales agents and customer service representatives are the busiest workers. After interviewing them about how they spend their time, you learn that up to three hours a day are spent logging customer calls, updating the CRM system, and filing expenses. After speaking with a temp agency, you find a temporary worker to help with sales and customer service support. This gives each sales and customer service representative an additional 2 hours per day, or 10 hours per week, to focus on Flashpoint 100.

Create Excitement and Fun

Creating energy, enthusiasm, and excitement is key. It doesn't have to be expensive, but it can make a huge difference when people feel energy in the air. Employees are more likely to help with Flashpoint 100, work harder, show up earlier, leave later, and put their heart and soul into what they do if they are enjoying the process. When times are tough, excitement helps them to stick it out. And when there are problems, employees are more motivated to find solutions and collaborate. Employees should feel that they are part of something *big*, and they have the opportunity to contribute directly to the company's success.

Most employees want to be challenged, given new opportunities to prove themselves, and have ownership of something. However, some employees focus merely on the task at hand, and will need more guidance on what needs to be done.

Make your employees crack a smile during the day. Jokes, updates, pictures, and funny quotes keep the atmosphere light and entertaining. Send jokes in emails, clips of comedians, or cartoons. Post a trivia of the day challenge with a small prize. Hang funny pictures on the walls and do a "caption this!" competition. Rewards, prizes, and gifts can be motivating as well, as long as they are not too lavish. Other rituals, such as a free dinner or a special treat each time they stay past a certain hour, can help increase motivation as well.

Scenario:

Overnight, you get some friends to help you decorate the office with fun posters, pictures, stickers, quotes and references, and notes of encouragement. The walls are lively and serve as a constant reminder that Flashpoint 100 is ongoing. Every morning you send a funny inspirational quote via email from a book that you got online. As you stumble across (clean!) comedy routines about relevant topics such as work or productivity, you send clips to employees. Some find them cheesy or corny, but most people get a kick out of it and it brings a smile to their face.

PART 4

HEAT

Nothing will work unless you do.

‒   Maya Angelou

Chapter 15
Putting it into Practice

Now it's time to implement the plans. The pre-work has been done. Issues and opportunities have been identified, ideas have been proposed, projects have been scoped and selected, costs have been allocated, and benefits forecast. From the big list of projects to do over the next few months, it's clear what everyone needs to do. This is where the hard work starts. Your employees are your greatest resource, so treat them as such.

This time also requires the most energy, motivation, and focus. The action steps are clearly defined because if there is an interruption or you need to stop for a while, it's possible to continue the project later without experiencing too many problems.

Communication

Since Flashpoint 100 will require so much of your company's time and energy, your employees need to know what to expect. This is a good time to begin all-staff meetings to introduce the process. Make sure functions have internal updates to better coordinate the projects they are leading and supporting. In these meetings, managers should remind everyone (briefly) of what the plan will achieve, and how far everyone is in the process. Make it interactive by featuring video or other multimedia, and inviting staff to ask each other questions and propose challenges.

Not Perfect, but Fit-for-Purpose

Keep in mind it's more important for projects to be executed efficiently than executed perfectly. In order to implement a large number of projects, you must sacrifice the idea of total perfection. One of the reasons projects are scoped in detail and progressively allocated resources is so that things cannot go too badly. So encourage employees to take risks and make decisions instead of waiting for detailed information or multiple levels of permission. Perfection can happen at a later stage, but now it is about pushing the boundaries to see what works.

Employees will attempt to accomplish their objectives, but often things don't go completely to plan. This is okay! It's better to understand whether or not the projects are worthwhile, if they can be accomplished, and if they are worth the resources and time to complete. As much as possible make action owners, project champions, and support teams aware that the end goal is more important than specific methods. Employees or team members shouldn't be punished for making decisions in good faith even if they turn out poorly.

Reporting lines is one example of the rules being relaxed in order to get more done. Some companies have strict policies on who has the authority to sign off on critical processes (i.e. expenses). In other cases, there are signoff requirements for things that are less critical. During the execution period, suspend unnecessary processes or documentation so that employees are freed where possible. Anything that requires multiple signoffs, permissions, or authority could be reviewed for streamlining during this time. To maintain a good line of sight on current events, managers can set clear expectations in advance on which critical processes to suspend. This way, employees know the difference between where there is wiggle room and where lines should not be crossed.

Scenario:

Typically, Marketing has to get all advertising spending signed off by the head of marketing, the head of branding, and the CFO. However, during Flashpoint 100, the CFO pre-approves a spend of $1,000 for marketing, and the head of branding signs off on any campaigns using pre-existing artwork or materials. The marketing team can now quickly execute a new campaign aimed at a slightly older customer segment to test product appeal, shaving two weeks off the turnaround time for the advertising placement.

Reaching the Finish Line

To ensure that the execution goes as smoothly as possible, maintain focus on how to do the projects efficiently, effectively, and with minimal impact on resources. Below are some tips.

1. **Eyes on the prize**—The end goal is achieving the super-objective and junior objectives. Specific projects will fall through, get delayed, pushed back, or cancelled, but that's not a problem as long as the overall tinderbox points toward achieving those all-important objectives.

2. **Keep going, no matter what**—Completion is key, not getting everything right. For this reason, place a big emphasis on solving problems as they come up, removing obstacles, and getting things back on track. Don't worry about getting the "perfect solution"—any solution allowing you to move quickly without significant costs is worth

pursuing. Some results are better than no results at the end of the 100-day period. Some projects will be cancelled for good reason. Make sure that a cancelled project is not due to unnecessary holdups: vacations, permissions, conflicting goals, low motivation, being forgotten, or scheduling conflicts.

3. **Don't sweat the small stuff**—It can be easy to get caught up in the details and worry about the specifics. Management, project champions, and team members should prioritize in order to make rapid decisions (within bounds) to ensure movement. Mistakes are unavoidable, but most should be forgivable. If a mistake is made, acknowledge it, make corrections where necessary, and move on.

4. **Tolerate failure**—Flashpoint 100 is designed for some things not to work. It is a natural part of trying something for the first time, and a necessary part of creativity. Many projects will not be completed, while others may be completed but fail to deliver the promised results. This is by design. Only by trying to do the impossible can you discover what is truly possible.

5. **It's not personal**—Make sure the team and project champions know that they are supported and valued, and that project failures will not be seen as personal failures as long as they put in the effort. This will encourage them to take the risks needed to make the projects work, and will promote creative problem-solving, which is essential to success.

Avoiding Fatigue

Flashpoint 100 is an intense process. At some point employees, management, and other stakeholders will get tired of the whole thing. They will regret the day that Flashpoint 100 ever began. This is normal, and one of the reasons that it doesn't stretch out beyond 100 days. By listening to issues that arise during the execution period, respecting people's limits, maintaining support and encouragement, keeping it fun, and keeping an eye on the main goal, you and your employees can maintain the energy needed to keep going.

Respect the Time Limits

It's easier to push really hard to complete something when the end is near, or when you know exactly what to expect. One thing that can make people lose motivation is when things drag on and it seems there is just no end in sight. In this area, monitoring can be quite powerful—projects missing their milestones can be pulled or reviewed. Do not let any project drag on past its deadlines without a good reason. When projects are given extended timelines, the justification can be communicated back to employees so that they understand that Flashpoint 100 is still being managed and monitored. Generally, when projects can't meet their milestones on time but still show promise, delay or suspend them until they can be resourced.

Stay Supportive . . . but Firm

When people have to work with each other in new ways, sometimes problems emerge. Perhaps sales employees are usually out of the office on sales calls, but now they are required to participate in weekly in-office meetings. Perhaps the web designer isn't used to strict deadlines, but is now told that something must be finished by a particular date. All of the new ways of working will require a new level of support, and there could be snafus that result in missed appointments, forgotten meetings, and data coming in late or wrong.

While getting these issues ironed out, it's important to stay supportive but firm so that people work together to get projects done. Ask what's needed to solve problems within the given parameters. Solicit feedback on how the projects could be resourced, monitored, and completed. The whole process runs only if employees and managers have enough time, space, permission, and resources to get things done. Strike a balance between permitting mistakes and failures, without tolerating a lack of effort.

Give Rewards

Rewards are great incentives for getting things done, and great at showing employees that you recognize their hard work and accomplishments, but don't overdo it. The real reward is seeing hard work and team efforts transform into big changes for the business. Other tools can help employees push through on the difficult days.

Employees can also plan their annual leave and holidays around Flashpoint 100 so that when it's over, the company can take a bit of a break. Giving non-critical employees an extra day or two off after Flashpoint 100 can also be a nice way to say thank you. Another way to thank the whole company is to reduce the hours or close the office (to non-critical employees) on a Friday or Monday.

A mix of pre-announced rewards and surprises that are arranged and planned at the beginning works well. These provide employees and other stakeholders with an incentive to work extra-hard, and help them visualize what they are working for. Make these rewards nice, memorable, and worthwhile, but not too lavish. Small rewards feel good to employees and show that you recognize the effort and accomplishment.

Give away small gifts on a scheduled and unexpected basis to lighten the mood and show your appreciation for employees' extra effort. Inexpensive gifts can work wonders: books, flowers, movie tickets, dinner vouchers, and lottery tickets or competitive prizes.

Employees usually claim that cash is very popular as a reward, but in reality cash rarely motivates people as much as non-cash rewards. If you reward employees with cash, keep it small (e.g., under $50) and stick to physical bills instead of a paycheck increase.

Gifts that rely on personal taste, such as perfume or clothing, are not recommended because people's tastes are subjective. Unless you know an employee's preferences, such as a favorite perfume, avoid these gifts. Experience-related gifts are usually very memorable and appreciated by anyone: cinema tickets, dinner-for-two vouchers, festival tickets, hotel stays, or other activities. For larger gifts, electronics and related gifts work well, like smartphones, tablets, game consoles, iTunes gift cards, and digital readers.

Charity donations are popular with some employees, and are naturally a very appropriate group reward. For instance, you can announce: "if 75 percent of our projects are on track at the end of the month, I will donate $1,000 to Charity X." For effectiveness, survey employees in advance about their favorite charities. Local charities that operate in or near the vicinity of the company are often good choices. If you can arrange for a charity representative to thank the company for the donation in person, that will make it even more memorable.

Scenario:

You realize that Flashpoint 100 is going to require long hours in the office for many employees, and you introduce several rituals. Every Wednesday afternoon there is a pizza party. Every Friday is the Weekend Raffle, where five employees receive gifts or weekend activity vouchers: a box of chocolates, cupcakes, cinema tickets, bowling vouchers, golf lessons, free yoga classes, concert tickets, free ice cream, passes for cooking classes, or cocktail mixing classes. You bought most of these on a daily deals site for 50% of their face value. Also, you institute a dinner rule: anytime people stay past 9:00 p.m., dinner is provided from a favorite local takeout place. These rewards do add up, but when you total up the employees' extra effort, they cost far less than a cash bonus or a salary raise.

Celebrate Successes

Achievements can also be rewarded by celebrating successes with big signs, all-employee bulletins of congratulations, or handwritten notes/cards handed to employees personally. Whenever a project finishes, mark the event with some kind of recognition, such as a group announcement.

Group events and parties are also great ways for people to unwind, relax, bond, and perhaps share strategies. For instance, in-office parties for people's birthdays, maternity leave departures, or a company outing to the go-cart track can be very popular. Employees look forward to them, and they can be a great way to celebrate group achievements and take a much-needed break. During that time, managers can also informally catch up with employees to check on the amount of time they are spending, any necessary rebalancing, and team chemistry. It also gives a chance for employees to network and understand more about others' projects.

Chapter 16
Monitoring

Why Monitor Projects?

Monitoring is the best way to know how well Flashpoint 100 is working. This is less about babysitting employees and more about clear decision-making and resource allocation. Frequent monitoring is a Flashpoint 100 hallmark allowing you to give additional support to a project that needs it. To help prevent slowdowns, each monitoring meeting is streamlined so that only the most relevant information is discussed, and decisions can be made quickly and easily.

How Much Monitoring is Enough?

Given the intensity level of Flashpoint 100 and the ambitious project deadlines, frequent monitoring is recommended. Two types of monitoring meetings are held at regular intervals. Each type has its own tracking sheet (see the Pulse Check and Checkpoint Review Templates at the back of the book) that will help minimize the meeting time and focus the discussion on the most critical points. For this reason, weekly and every-three-week meetings keep projects from getting derailed before problems are noticed. These checks allow you to quickly see how Flashpoint 100 is progressing.

Other types of meetings can be held ad hoc or when a natural milestone is reached. For instance, when a vendor sends a quote for materials for a new product idea, it's a natural decision point on whether to continue pursuing the idea or cancelling it. Dealing with it as it comes is sometimes better than waiting for days until the next meeting.

When problems do emerge, it's good to review the areas that need additional support. If done in a group setting, broad problems can be brainstormed to see if others can help do problem solving, or volunteer their time to help.

How to Monitor Progress

Flashpoint 100 has two recommended regular methods for monitoring progress: Pulse Checks and Checkpoints.

Pulse Checks—Weekly

The Pulse Check is a weekly update meeting, and the best monitoring system to spot problems early on. Hold weekly Pulse Check meetings as efficiently as possible and with a standard information template (see the Pulse Check Template in the Templates section at the back of the book). The ideal Pulse Check takes 5–20 minutes, and simply reviews the status of a project. Each week, the project champion should update the tool with what has been accomplished and what has not.

Don't get too bogged down with lots of data entry and logging information, but issue simple updates based on what has been agreed in the Project Profile. If you are good at Microsoft Excel, build the template in Excel and simply change the pull-down menus. Visit www.Flashpoint100.com for templates and other content to help support you. Data entry on a weekly basis should take 15–20 minutes maximum for each project. Prior to the data entry, the project champion and activity owners should discuss the status of each activity face-to-face or via email.

A day before the Pulse Check meeting, ask employees to fill out the tool and submit it. During the meeting, focus on highlighting the areas that are off track or need more support. Short meetings work for projects that are either progressing quickly or are on track. Even if a project is going according to plan, hold the Pulse Check meeting, because simply getting in front of the project champion and reviewing progress helps ensure that any unaddressed issues surface.

In principle, the Pulse Check meeting should be done one-on-one. In addition to reviewing the Pulse Check update, request backup and documentation for some of the on-track projects. The goal is to promote truthfulness and ensure a shared understanding of on-track measures. As a manager, it's important to see not just *what* was done but *how*—for instance, which agreements were made with suppliers, or what the schedule for a new media plan will be.

While you are speaking to the project champion during the Pulse Check, take notes directly onto the Pulse Check Template to avoid transferring notes from one place to another. The template can feed directly into the next week's plans and goals, which minimizes the amount of notes to review the following week.

If you have done a good job at writing the Project Profile, then each action has a clear deadline. Also, by each monitoring meeting, a list of things should have been accomplished if the project is going well. Focus on things that are out of line with the project profile: missed deadlines, the key employee's inability to handle the workload, a cost overrun, or a newly discovered market opportunity. Any expectations that should be changed can also factor in to updates of the Project Profiles. For instance, if a product is not selling as well as it did before, revenue expectations can be adjusted downwards. The monitoring will allow you to answer questions like: Are we on track? Has something gone terribly wrong? Could we use additional resources? Monitoring is critical for finding and addressing problems early on.

Scenario:

One of the Flashpoint 100 projects is to change the payment provider for the website. Right now you are paying a fee of 3 percent of all payments made through the site, the same as when it was set up two years ago. However, now you're doing more business and you think you can get a better rate with another provider. A financial analyst is the project champion, and you meet with him weekly on the progress of the changeover. The project is on track, with different providers assessed and an initial cost analysis done. He submits information from the different payment providers in advance, and during the Pulse Check meeting you discuss any non-financial considerations, like trust in the brand. The meeting takes 10 minutes, and he gets the go-ahead to continue with the project.

Checkpoints—Every Three Weeks

Checkpoints are regular, large-forum meetings that happen with senior management and project champions. The goal is to communicate any progress that's been made on the projects, invite discussion and insight into further action, and get objective feedback on effective and ineffective measures. The two main goals of a Checkpoint meeting are to make a Go or No-Go decision on each project, and to reallocate resources where necessary. Afterward, projects can be given the budget they were allocated, more or less budget than they were allocated, or they can be cancelled.

Do Checkpoints every three weeks, which allows for four to five Checkpoints during Flashpoint 100. This is frequent enough to catch any problems before they get out of hand, but not so frequent that decisions aren't meaningful. Use the Project Profile Template in the back of the book to capture information and decisions on projects, and to help guide the meeting.

Pulse Checks feed into Checkpoints, giving an informed view of what's working and what isn't. Do Pulse Checks and Checkpoints in-office and face-to-face if possible. Keep them a bit more formal so they are taken seriously. For this reason, avoid doing them in a distracting environment such as a production floor. Everyone should be able to concentrate and focus on the task at hand to make the meeting as efficient as possible.

The Schedule for Pulse Checks and Checkpoints

As recommended earlier, regular Checkpoints to review progress will highlight problems early on, and let you as a manager decide what to do with them. Apart from cancelling, there are other options for projects that don't meet their Checkpoint requirements. People can be put on other projects, money can be reduced, and the project itself can be delayed until more information is gathered or other projects are done. Each Checkpoint should be attended by senior management and by the relevant project champions. Do evaluations with results from the Pulse Checks (including any highlighted projects that were doing very well or very poorly). If projects stay on track without experiencing any problems, and new projects or opportunities do not come up, use the Checkpoint system:

- *Checkpoint 1—Go/No-Go*—on Day 14, the completed plan is presented and approved by management and the board. On this day, target an allocation of about 25 to 50 percent of the total money or resources requested by each project.

- *Checkpoint 2*—around Day 35, this review should target a release of another 25 percent of resources requested by a project.

- *Checkpoint 3*—at roughly Day 56, this review should target about 25 percent of resources requested by a project.

- *Checkpoint 4*—at about Day 77, this review should release the remaining funds that projects require.

Scenario:

The Flashpoint 100 started on January 1. After the initial planning and scoping, 22 projects were given the go-ahead for implementation. At each Checkpoint, projects were cancelled or stopped based on their performance. By the end of Flashpoint 100, on day 98, eight projects were completed.

Remaining projects by date

Day	Date	Checkpoint #	Remaining projects
Day 14	15-Jan	Checkpoint 1	22
Day 35	5-Feb	Checkpoint 2	15
Day 56	26-Feb	Checkpoint 3	11
Day 77	19-Mar	Checkpoint 4	9
Day 98	9-Apr	Final meeting	8

The Dashboard

Monitoring the status of all projects can be done with a simple tool called the Dashboard (see Dashboard Template in the back of the book). The Dashboard tracks the number of projects in progress, their status, the current amount spent, and the remaining amount to be allocated. Updated after each Pulse Check, it's a great way to keep track of things so you can review the progress of Flashpoint 100 at a moment's notice.

Time-Outs—as Needed

If a project is salvageable but has run into real problems, time-outs can put the project on hold while issues are sorted out. Assign team members and action owners to support other projects while the issue gets sorted. Employees, management, or other stakeholders can also call a time-out if something needs to be reviewed, additional resources need to be received, or a problem needs to be solved. Encourage calling time-outs as early as possible so issues can be reviewed and addressed before they tie up precious resources and create drag on employee motivation.

In addition, the company can call a time-out on the whole Flashpoint 100. A client crisis, an investment offer, or a lawsuit could require the time and attention of the full company for a while. Don't be afraid to pause what's been done so you can pick it up later. One of the reasons the Activities section of Project Profile is so detailed is to be able to pick it up later if you need a break.

Sprints—as Needed

During other times, a particular project may require nearly everyone's time for a short period. For instance, if you are speaking and exhibiting at a conference, Marketing may need to prepare materials, Sales may need to attend and target prospective customers, Production might provide special samples and giveaways, and Administration might oversee logistics and manning the booth. For these few days, it's fine if Flashpoint 100 is put on hold so everyone can support a joint effort.

Other projects may create spikes in activity from other functions. For instance, if Marketing creates a major new social media campaign, it may create a flood of inquiries to Customer Service and Sales, and a higher demand on Product Management and Operations. Most of these can be anticipated and worked into the project profile before the execution phase begins.

❀❖❁

Chapter 17
Firefighting

What Could Go Wrong?

During the execution phase, many things could go wrong. Common problems include lack of data, cost overruns, agencies or partners not fulfilling their roles, etc. The execution process itself is designed to highlight and incorporate issues so that projects can be fast-tracked or cancelled.

How to Spot a Problem

The first indicator that something is wrong is in the regular Pulse Check meeting. This is why these are so important. When the employee or manager sits to down to review progress, any off-track projects can be immediately identified. There is often a very good reason, so it's important to be supportive in the discussion and to give the employee the benefit of the doubt wherever possible.

Begin by having a frank and open conversation where the project champion is encouraged to highlight any issues with you. Instead of just marking something as on-track or off-track, identify how the progress has gone and review the assumptions underlying the initiative. As much as possible, avoid blame or finger-pointing, but do try to understand whether the problem originates at the team level or with an external party. Perhaps the person is in over their head and needs a bit more guidance or support to develop the initiative. Perhaps they simply have too many things on their plate and the initiative is taking up too much time and effort. Also, the timing of the most carefully-planned initiative can be derailed by events like unexpected absences, employee departures, and client crises.

You don't have to wait to discuss the situation with an employee. Encouraging your employees to come to you as issues develop can prevent problems cropping up all at once. Even with weekly Pulse Checks, losing several days of productivity (due to a delay) can affect the Flashpoint 100 timelines.

Knowing Which Problems to Fix

When deciding which problems to fix, weigh the effort, time, and cost required to fix the problem against the benefits of solving it. Try to reach the heart of what isn't working and target those issues. Problems worth fixing can be handled without compromising the company's ability to deliver in other ways.

Fixable problems typically fall into one of several categories.

- **Capacity problems** are related to the team's inability to implement the project due to lack of experience, knowledge, or time. Find ways to re-staff these projects, give greater support (more people), or longer timelines.
- **Resource problems** crop up when needs and resources are mismatched. This could be due to incorrect estimates of the amount of a resource needed to successfully execute an initiative, such as an advertising campaign. Sometimes suppliers change their estimates based on changes to their prices or quotes based on your needs. For these, consider giving greater resources. However, update the benefit analysis on the project to make sure it still makes sense given more resources.

- **Scoping problems** arise when a project needs to be redesigned or when expectations get changed. Perhaps more approvals are needed to launch a new product, or a new product needs special packaging. These types of problems suggest that the project should be re-scoped and resourced accordingly. Make sure the new team has a full understanding of the requirements.

In other cases, certain things simply fail, and this is normal. For instance, an attempt to renegotiate a lease with a landlord may be unsuccessful. Flashpoint 100 is designed to attempt more projects than are possible to accomplish, to make sure no stone is left unturned and the company is doing everything possible to achieve results.

After further consideration, some projects may just not be a good idea because of the level of competition or the project's effect on the company. Maybe a much larger competitor has just dropped its price, or the new product idea would attract a high level of regulatory scrutiny. Certain projects like these will require gut decisions, not just profit analysis.

In general, Game-Changer projects need more support and guidance. They often become more complex over time, requiring clear documentation and component tracking. Be prepared to have a backup plan on these, such as alternative relocation sites, to make sure the viable ones are pushed through.

If the project requires more money or people to make it happen, put it on a special review list.

Scenario:
One Game-Changer project requires adding a factory production line. After careful research by the project champion, a machine has is identified that fits the criteria for the product, but the supplier no longer manufactures the machines. The project is about to be cancelled when a production supervisor thinks to check online and sees a used one for sale in Argentina. However, this will take several weeks to carry out, and will require a site

---

visit to ensure that the machine is functional. After reviewing the numbers, the additional costs and time will be offset by the savings and greater efficiency, so the new solution is given the go-ahead.

When to Cancel a Project

Cancel a project due to execution problems only after you are satisfied that the problems are not fixable, or worth fixing. To do this, get enough information on what is not working; make sure you are confident that you have been given the full story. Once you've made the decision, communicate it quickly to the team and rest of the function, and update the documents. Do this in a blameless way, without pinning the decision on the failure of any person, team, or function.

Keep in mind that the money that has been spent is just that—spent. You can't get back those sunk costs, even by pushing a project forward. Don't cling to a project that isn't going to work just because of what has been done so far. If it won't work, it won't work.

Scenario:
The Marketing team was very excited about a new social media campaign targeted at younger customers. However, a month of executing the campaign has brought lackluster results. Originally the campaign was estimated to cost $2,000 and so far, $1,000 has been spent on the social media agency's first payment and the online advertising costs. With virtually no uptick in customers from this segment, you cancel the social media project, even though you won't get a refund from the agency.

Chapter 18
Reallocating Resources

Tight management of resources is critical to performance of Flashpoint 100. Cash is one of the biggest—but not the only—resources to manage. Other resources, including people's time and assets, should be given to projects only when earned.

Reallocation Triggers

There are three main ways to decide when to reallocate resources: with new information, after a cancellation, or with an unexpected opportunity.

New Information

Sometimes, new information changes the project's chance of success. This new information could be related to government regulations, competitors, customer behavior, technological platforms, or anything else that affects a project's chances. This could also include anything that was overlooked at the beginning when the project was scoped.

When new information arrives, flag it and examine it for relevance. Call a time-out on the relevant project until the information can be incorporated into the planning for the project.

Allocating Resources after a Cancellation

Once a project is cancelled, its earmarked resources can be allocated to other projects or kept as savings. If you would like to allocate them to other projects, ensure that these other projects have met their milestones or are due to deliver a big benefit from additional resources. For instance, if a Facebook advertising campaign is cancelled due to poor performance but a Google AdWords campaign yields good results, transfer the money earmarked for Facebook into the Google account.

Unexpected Opportunities

Occasionally, opportunities appear that could make a big difference to the company. These could be one-time-only discounts from a supplier, or an asset sale from a competitor that is exiting your line of business. Retaining some cash allows you to make these types of decisions much more quickly.

Apart from cash, it's important to constantly review the time and activities of key support people. Often these people are in Marketing, Sales, Administration, and Finance. Their job is to oversee or implement marketing or packaging changes, sell new products or offer new services, create meetings and events, organize new business processes, process expenses, or procure new equipment. As projects are activated or cancelled, the time and placement of these people should be considered as well.

Ω❖Ω

Chapter 19
Secrets of Successful Execution

Flashpoint 100 is intense and challenging to pull off. Keeping your focus on the six principles below will help you complete Flashpoint 100 to standard and within budget, with a lot to show for it.

1. Steady Focus

Staying focused means prioritizing Flashpoint 100 on a day-to-day basis, encouraging others to make it a priority, and maintaining a high level of energy. While dozens of tempting new possibilities and opportunities may arise during this time, it's important to really push them aside in order to focus on Flashpoint 100. Putting off potential partners, new business requests, or other opportunities for a few months may sound difficult, but realistically, you are making these kinds of decisions on a regular basis.

One reason Flashpoint 100 is just 100 days is that it's easier to maintain focus until the goal is reached. Any time period longer than that and people begin to get weary. Creating the energy and excitement of Flashpoint 100 also does a lot to ensure that the goal stays fresh in people's minds. Regular communication, celebrating wins, rewarding success, and posting goals in a visible place also help people remember why they are doing all of this work.

However, some too-good-to-miss opportunities should be considered. The question to ask yourself is: based on this new opportunity, which projects (of a similar size or aim) *am I willing to stop*? You will have to make trade-offs. If the opportunity does not stack up against killing a similar project, then don't do it. It's that simple.

Scenario:

On Day 55, an investor brings you an opportunity: a small competitor has run into financial difficulties and is looking for a buyer for the company right away. Evaluating the project would take about 30 days' worth of site visits, analyzing the competitor's business, market research, and talks with legal and investment advisors. If it's a good deal, it could extend your product set into an important segment.

Currently, you have 20 projects ongoing, 2 of which are Game-Changers: a new product and an office relocation. Reviewing the three, you decide that the office relocation is not critical at the moment. Therefore, you drop that project and pursue the competitor buy-out instead.

---

2. Regular Pulse Checks and Checkpoints

Regular Pulse Checks and Checkpoints have several benefits. They help tell you when something is wrong or needs to be addressed with, say, more resources. The Pulse Checks and Checkpoints also serve as a reminder to the company that Flashpoint 100 is an important priority for everyone. When employees aren't asked how they are doing on a project, they begin to question its importance. You need to send the signal that what they are doing is necessary and valuable, and will transform the company.

For this reason and others, continue having Checkpoints and Pulse Checks even when everything seems fine. Even if they are repetitive or the project champions have little to report, simply saying "no change—still on track" is useful. It helps to maintain accountability.

Checkpoints and Pulse Checks also serve as a way for you to check the mood of your employees and see whether they have any other concerns. These conversations can be very fruitful because you get a chance to interact on a regular basis with them, outside of the realm of their day-to-day jobs. This helps you get to know them in other settings and see how they understand you, communicate, finish activities, and learn.

3. Clear Accountabilities

On a volleyball team, there are six players on the court, and each plays a specific position. If the team is disorganized or not paying attention, the ball can fly to their side and fall, untouched, smack in the middle of the court. Even worse, sometimes everyone on the team takes a little step back to allow someone else to get it, then watches in horror as the ball hits the ground. This problem is common in amateur teams; when no one sees the ball as their responsibility, no one moves to take control of it. In contrast, professional volleyball players communicate who should get the ball, and if there is any ambiguity, everyone dives for it.

Flashpoint 100 works in a similar way. Each action has an owner, and each project has a champion. Function heads should be very familiar with the number, shape, and size of the projects within their function. This prevents people from thinking that a project will be taken care of by someone else, or that their responsibility is limited, since it is a shared task. Although goals, benefits, and costs should be shared, activities and project champion roles should not.

Assigning action-owners makes it much easier for Pulse Check and Checkpoint discussions, since each meeting will be held with a single action-owner, or possibly a team of people who are action-owners. Trying to have meetings with multiple people is much more complex, and there is the possibility of the blame game. To avoid this scenario, assign clear accountabilities so there is always someone who owns the job of being on the ball. You can discuss resourcing and cancellation decisions directly with that person without having to consult a larger group.

Scenario:

One of the Low-Hanging Fruit projects involves renegotiating with the landlord on the rent. Every week you meet with the project champion to discuss progress—whether any documents have been submitted, whether the landlord is asking for anything in return, etc.

By contrast, one of the Game-Changers involves a decision on whether or not to set up a regional office near one of your major clients in São Paolo, Brazil. The project champion is the COO, but each Pulse Check also features the head of marketing, the CFO, and the head of sales, since they are critically involved in the development and decision-making. Although they each answer to the COO, some of your questions are so complex that you prefer to have each of them in the room.

---

4. Factoring in Linkages and Dependencies

Sometimes projects fail due to insufficient support by the support team, which could be any function (e.g. Marketing, Production, Sales, Finance) that is critical to a successful project implementation.

In these instances, a project fails just because the supporting team didn't have enough capacity to implement it.

In many cases, specific activities or responsibilities are linked. For instance, Production may need to increase inventory before Marketing can release a new marketing campaign, or else you risk running embarrassing stock shortages. Finance and Procurement may need to sign off on new suppliers, and this gets delayed, then the new production inputs don't arrive in time for the production schedule. Failing to realize these needs in advance of a project can mean unnecessary delays if the support team receives a last-minute request they can't accommodate. Understanding the link between each function and the task, and preparing by scoping the project accordingly, reduces these types of risks.

For each project, and across the tinderbox as a whole, identify the linkages and dependencies in advance, and factor those in as needed.

5. Prototyping and Trial and Error

Trying things out for the first time can be a challenge. Even if you're absolutely confident things will go a certain way, they almost never do. Sometimes you will get happy surprises, but sometimes the surprises will be nasty.

Prototyping and trial and error are critical to protect the company from the negative surprises of doing something for the first time. This means finding ways to experiment before putting full project resources behind it. This is going to be especially important for Game-Changers and Meat and Potatoes projects.

Prototyping means creating a mock-up of an idea to be tested with partners or customers. Instead of manufacturing a batch of the new phone accessory you want to sell, see if a local 3-D printing partner can do a prototype (or two) that can be used in discussions with distributors. In the very early days, you can use designs or renderings with customers for initial testing to get a sense of what works and what doesn't. This allows you to make improvements and begin targeting customer segments prior to a full rollout of the product.

6. Problem-Solving

Two other keys to success involve putting out fires and problem-solving. Please keep in mind that you won't always make the "right" decision. Speed and moving projects forward is more important than being detailed. At this stage, it's better to make mistakes than to risk delaying worthy projects and pushing things back.

Examples of tolerable mistakes include things like quoting a supplier a price that is too low, or buying too much inventory. Rather than tie up resources or spending weeks settling on a detail, be speedy and resourceful. If you are worried about big mistakes that could affect the company, think about ways to put in place temporary contracts or language that allows cancellations. Decide in advance the No-Go areas and make those known. For example, a No-Go area might be a contract longer than a year, or approving an expense larger than $1,000 without the CFO's approval.

Scenario:

The Marketing team has come up with a project profile that includes releasing clever online videos, and it's targeted to produce $3,000 in earnings. After getting quotes from marketing agencies to produce the custom videos, the lowest cost was $4,000. This would eat up all of the earnings and make it unviable.

Instead, you find a freelancer with pre-designed animation characters that can be customized. You decide to redo the campaign to fit one of the characters as a "spokesperson." The campaign animations cost a total of $1,000, and they are impressive, although not the same quality as the full videos. However, it's still a great representation of the brand.

---

෫ ❖ ෮

PART 5

IGNITE

Thunder is good, thunder is impressive;
but it is lightning that does the work.

– Mark Twain

Chapter 20
The Final Analysis and Meeting

B y now, you have completed the last Checkpoint, and you have the final list of projects that will be completed during Flashpoint 100. Over these last six days, focus on wrapping things up, getting feedback, collecting data, and making final decisions on what to push forward.

Pulse Check

The final Pulse Check is a bit different from the others. Unlike previous Pulse Checks that assessed if projects were on track or not, now you know the status of each one. Shift focus to getting data and details for a number of specific things:

- Actions that were not completed, and why
- Whether the project will be completed on time and if not, why not
- Total final costs of the project
- Total quantitative benefits realized so far (e.g., the number of additional customers, additional revenue, cost savings, etc.)

- Total qualitative benefits so far (e.g., better communication, more efficient processes, less time wasted, more clarity on roles), with examples where possible

Analysis

DAYS 95–97

Now it's time to do the final analysis—what worked, what didn't, and what's happened so far. To do this effectively, you need to understand what happened during the process. This can be accomplished by some simple yet powerful analyses, aimed at summarizing the activity during Flashpoint 100, and understanding the results.

There are four analyses to do in the final week.

Process Analysis—Understanding How Well the Process Worked

Understanding the process and its impact on the company can place the results in context, and also give some valuable information about your company. The process analysis is done first because it sets the scene for other analyses later on. The process analysis reveals if Flashpoint 100 worked as expected, the amount of effort that was expended, and whether or not there was a good match of projects to responsibilities.

Don't spend too much time on the process analysis, since it will be a high-level summary based on your impressions, and the notes that you took. Review the notes from Pulse Check and Checkpoint meetings to get a better sense of themes and trends; which projects sailed through the process, which projects got stuck, which functions were particularly successful, any reasons for these functions' success, etc.

These are some questions to consider for the process analysis:
- Did people work together well, or did they compete and withhold information or support?
- Did people go above and beyond their usual level of effort?
- Where was the planning insufficient or inappropriate?

- Where was money, time, or effort wasted?
- Who surprised you with what they were able to accomplish?
- Who disappointed you with what they did not get done?
- Where was the process too ambitious?
- How much extra time did the staff spend working?
- Which types of projects did especially well?
- Which types of projects did especially poorly?

The purpose of the process analysis is to measure the final results against the effort and the capabilities of your company. This helps you better understand the company's performance under pressure, and areas of weakness where you can put additional people or resources to get things done. Flashpoint 100 can reveal a lot about weaknesses and blind spots that could hurt the development of the Game-Changers later on.

Scenario:

Flashpoint 100 has been completed and you decide to examine how the Company Diagnostic looks now vs. when you first did it. You spent a bit more than you originally forecast, but the company is doing better and added a lot of new customers. You write in the levels to compare the first Company Diagnostic in Chapter 6 to today.

Company Diagnostic		
Area	**Description of Change**	**Level After F100**
Baseline performance	Sales skyrocketed over the last 3 months, and we added another 100 customers.	−Total units sold: 700 −Revenues: $700k −1-Yr Rev. growth: 25% −Cost of sales: $300k −Gross profit: $400k −Gross profit %: 57% −Fixed costs: $225k −Earnings: $175k −Cash in bank: $20k −W'king capital: $5k −Total spent on Flashpoint 100: $27k

---

Area	Description of Change	Level After F100
Business Model	Direct and indirect- via web and sales (face to face). Indirect sales is now a small proportion.	−N/A
Marketplace	No change.	−N/A
Competition	We've managed to steal a number of new customers from StreamLine due to our superior service and a targeted sales campaign. Competition is a strength.	−N/A
Products	Most customers have moved onto the all-in-one package, and the HR packages now are entry points. Prices have increased on all products with no loss of sales.	**Prices** −All-in-one pkg: $250/mo. −HR resume: $25/mo. −HR performance: $25 mo. −HR health costs: $75 mo.
Marketing	We've increased our overall digital marketing budget and focused most of it on AdWords.	−Monthly spend (avg.): $3k
Target customers	Small business owners with 50 employees or less, and 20 customers on a larger custom package with better pricing.	−350 monthly subscribers to the all-in-one package
Gaining & Retaining Customers	New customers only get a free 2-week trial, no first month free. A loyalty program has improved retention and grown new customer numbers.	−Gaining: $150 in foregone revenue −Retaining: free upgrades for loyal customers, referral bonus
Sales & Distribution	Website sales have grown to $200,000 annually, and are on track to be the majority in 2 years.	−Avg. sales/salesperson: $250k −Avg. compensation/salesperson: $100k
Company	One office, headquartered in Seattle, WA. Senior management includes the CEO, CFO, & CTO.	− N/A
Employees	We hired 4 new employees in Marketing, Customer Support, and Admin. We also reduced headcount in Tech by 1. The addition in Admin supports me with	−23 employees: −CEO (Me) −Finance−2 −Marketing−3 −Sales−2

Area	Description of Change	Level After F100
	special projects and project implementation.	−Cust. support−7 −Tech/ product development−5 −Admin/office−4
Operations	No material change.	−1 office −Account with Amazon Web Services (server space)
Partners	One partnership with Prestige Partners, and a new one with Advanta Consulting.	−2 partners- consulting (face-to-face sales) −They take a 20% commission
Technology & Assets	Early stages of developing a framework for licensing the existing patents that will be obsolete in the next upgrade.	−3 software patents −Brand trademark (name and logo in USA)
Biggest risks	The website problem is solved. New risks are related to failing at the new projects.	−N/A
Culture	Technology and Marketing work closely together on product upgrades and releases. Sales gives regular feedback from customers. Communication has improved dramatically.	−N/A

Like the first time, spend a short amount of time filling in the Company Diagnostic. The point is to capture the main changes, not do a detailed analysis.

Scenario:

Flashpoint 100 is almost done, and eight projects are nearing the finish line in nine days. You are about to calculate the benefits and costs to each of them, but first you review your notes from Pulse Checks and Checkpoints to see the problem areas of the process. In analyzing which projects did well and which ones experienced problems, you see a pattern: Marketing and Sales worked together seamlessly on several projects, significantly increasing customer orders. However, many of these orders were not delivered in full or on time, and some customers cancelled and went to the competition. It turns out that Production never adjusted their staffing schedule to accommodate the increased demand. One of the Game-Changers that will be submitted for approval involves a new product line that would require adding capacity by 20 percent. You make a note to work closely with Production to ensure that the employee availability matches the capacity needs.

Project Analysis

The project analysis is a simple one; by function, it shows the number of projects started and completed.

Scenario:
Each project is listed by function, and it shows that Administration had the highest number of completed projects. You know that most of these were Low-Hanging Fruit, so you're not concerned.

Function	Projects Started	Projects completed	Superstar champions?
Marketing	9	3	Joe Jackson, Marketing Mgr
Sales	12	6	Lara Reid, Business Development Mgr
Finance	4	3	Tony Lopez, Comptroller
Production	7	3	Mo Haddad, Head of Production
HR	2	2	N/A
Admin	14	11	Tom Collins, Executive Assistant

Projects completed

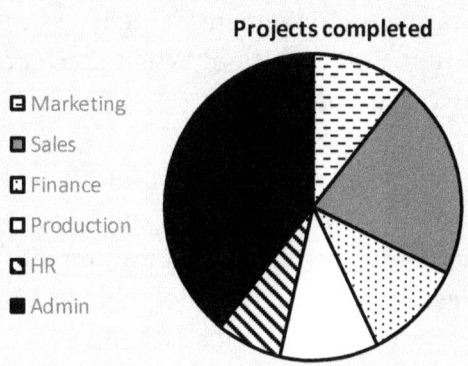

- Marketing
- Sales
- Finance
- Production
- HR
- Admin

Quantitative Analysis

The most straightforward impact to measure is quantitative; total costs, increases in revenue, increases in earnings, and so on. Quantitative data includes anything that can be measured using numbers: customers, orders, sales, costs, price, units, etc. If you started well at the beginning of the process, the Quantitative Analysis is easy to do with only a few metrics to collect. If you use the tool in the back of the book (the Dashboard Template), the calculations will be done automatically and quickly. At the beginning, you chose a super-objective (e.g., profit) to measure everything against. This makes it easier to calculate the total impact, and makes everything apples to apples.

It's common to work with Finance/Accounting on this analysis to ensure proper numbers and correct analysis. Going forward, Finance/Accounting should own the metrics and monitoring, so involve them in this process—ask what they need to make this happen. Finance/Accounting should have many of these numbers at their fingertips: increases in revenue, increases in costs, and changes to gross margin. You may need to work with them closely to separate out the project costs and spending.

Qualitative Benefits Analysis

Qualitative benefits are also worth tracking and analyzing, even if they can't be assigned a revenue or profit figure. Most companies are driven by qualitative achievements such as motivation, alignment, communication, and ambition. When these are present, companies are more successful over time.

Review the qualitative benefits from Flashpoint 100. The targets will have been identified in the very beginning, and updated during Pulse Checks and Checkpoints. Just like the beginning of Flashpoint 100 planning, be as specific as possible on the changes made from before, and ways that you can tell those changes. To measure whether it's specific, think of whether five people would agree on the assessment.

These are five common areas to review for qualitative changes.

- **Professionalism**—As companies grow, they often struggle with putting processes in place that can be repeated consistently, taught to new people, or otherwise make the company more professional. Professional companies have processes that are clearly understood and make the company run better, with consistency between different divisions and products.
- **Communication**—The hallmark of a professional company is its communication of relevant information to the right people. When employees are proactive about sharing knowledge with relevant stakeholders in a timely fashion, everyone can do their jobs much better.
- **Collaboration**—Most companies have people who are only used to working within their own teams. Learning to collaborate with other functions and people can be a great way to produce innovative solutions, refine existing ideas, and get support from others.
- **Alignment**—The alignment of strategy, tactics, and planning makes a company more efficient and more productive with less overall effort. It keeps everyone pulling in the same direction
- **Information capture, storage, and use**—For many companies, information management is a big issue. Customer details get lost, market intelligence gets misfiled, and best practices get forgotten. Better data capture, storage, and usage can be critical to generating more sales, taking better care of customers, and avoiding wasted effort due to repeated actions. Initiatives that increase the flow of data and information sharing, such as regular customer insight meetings, can be the difference between a mediocre company and a superstar. One secret is to choose the key

metrics and information that make the biggest difference — usually related to revenues, customers, costs, or efficiency.

Scenario:

Prior to Flashpoint 100, all customer invoices were generated by Jim in Finance, after Sales delivered paper order forms to his desk. Invoicing didn't happen until the salesperson delivered the form and Jim processed it. If a salesperson forgot to walk the form to Jim, or if Jim was on vacation, the invoice didn't get sent. Once, an invoice did not get sent until six months after delivery, when a salesperson cleaned out his desk and found an old order form. Two projects in Flashpoint 100 addressed this backlog. The first project tied sales commissions to invoice payments as well as signed orders. The second project set up an accounting system that automatically generated an invoice as soon as Distribution made a delivery. Now, invoices get sent out the same day that products are delivered, invoices are not getting misplaced, and customers are paying faster.

Scenario:

All data has been collected and turned into an earnings metric. This means that you have factored in ongoing costs but not project costs. Subtracting the project costs gives you a net project profit for each function, as well as the total. By adding up all the projects in Flashpoint 100, you get to $20,000 in net profit so far. The biggest profit drivers are Marketing, Sales, and Finance, due to their campaigns in advertising, sales, and accounts receivable. Production replaced several machines which will ultimately save costs. The other functions have a negative project profit because they don't generate sales, but they do promote qualitative benefits such as collaboration and communication. Breaking it down by function, you can see how each function contributes.

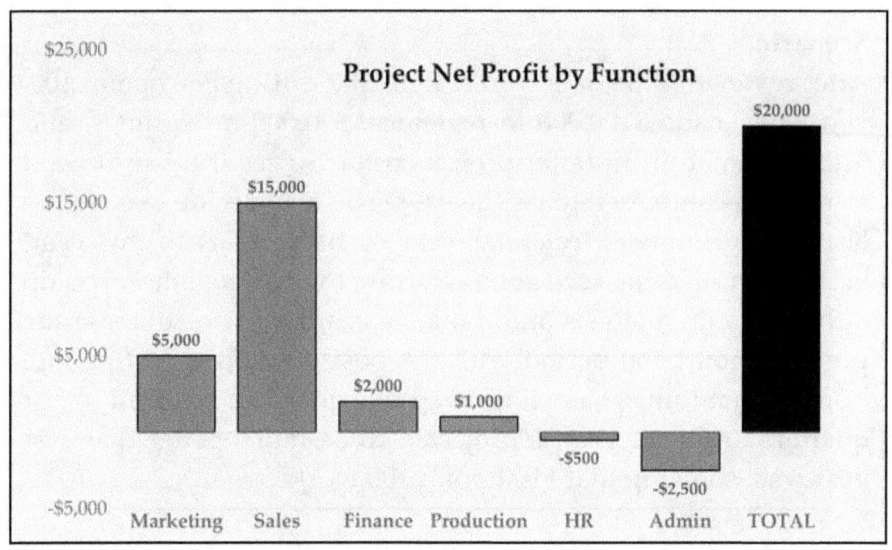

Avoiding Analysis Paralysis

Most of the insights can be determined by simple calculations and presented using clear graphics. At this point, avoid any temptation to spend days slicing and dicing the data from every different angle. If you want to know more detail on which products' sales grew the most, you can certainly capture that data and track it regularly. Also, many of the projects in Flashpoint 100 will have their own metrics. For instance, a project to launch a new product might count the percentage of current customers that bought the new product, or the product's brand recognition.

If you are highly analytical and enjoy playing with data and doing spreadsheets and calculations, feel free to go into more detailed analyses than those mentioned. Instead of estimates, use actual values for areas like new customers, gross margin broken down by type of product sold, or even gross margin by different distribution channels.

Scenario:

After reviewing the data, you realize that during Flashpoint 100, you have made $100,000 in revenues, $30,000 in earnings, and $20,000 in net profit (after project costs). To see if this is a good trend, you compare it to last quarter. You also decide to compare last year's numbers (calendar year or fiscal year) to this year, based on how things are going. Putting the two together, you do a three-month analysis and a one-year analysis to compare the pre-Flashpoint 100 period with the post-Flashpoint 100 period. You see that things have improved this quarter compared to last quarter. And next year is projected to be much better than last year was, showing that Flashpoint 100 worked well.

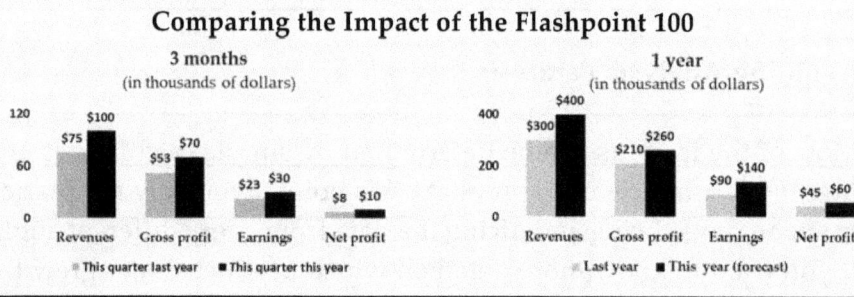

Comparing the Impact of the Flashpoint 100

Scenario:

You run a wholesale drinking water company. All Flashpoint 100 charts have been finalized, but something looks odd: you sold 20 percent more bottles of water this quarter, yet revenues were flat. You didn't drop the price—in fact, you raised it slightly—so you decide to investigate. After talking to Sales, you see that they signed up many new customers using a promotional discount. However, because many of these sales were long-term contracts and their future orders will be at full price, you are not worried about the flat revenues.

Final Wrap-Up and Presentations

DAYS 98–100

The Final Wrap-Up

Once the analysis is finished, you have a full picture of the impact of Flashpoint 100 and the company's financial position as a result. If you've used the templates in this book or developed some of your own, you now have simple charts that summarize the impact of Flashpoint 100 and how your business will grow. Take a step back, take a deep breath, and take stock. Was it worth it? How much did you gain? If you followed Flashpoint 100 closely, you probably experienced something like this:

- **Surprise**—your employees amazed you with how much they were able to accomplish in such a short period of time, and you wonder how they can reach that same level of commitment at other times of the year.
- **Verification**—a number of projects seemed to work despite your skepticism, while other seemingly promising projects were disappointing.
- **Perspective**—after quite a lot of "wasted" money in the first part of the process, you now see that stopping these projects early on prevented you from wasting more money in the future.
- **Employees**—you identified your employee superstars and the underperformers, and in general, employees have taken greater ownership of their responsibilities in the company (more initiative, more proactivity, and more ideas).
- **Culture**—the company is more professional, better-managed, and with better lines of communication. You hope that the new habits stick with employees.
- **Game-Changers**—one or two major new projects look very doable. You are confident that investing your money, time, effort, and reputation in these projects will yield very good results because you have found a customer base that is enthusiastic and suppliers that are reliable. You are ready to

present these proposals to the board or the decision-makers for their approval. With the high quality of the proposals and potential for good returns, there is an excellent chance they will agree to it all.

This is normal. Flashpoint 100 is not designed for everything to work out perfectly; it's designed to make experimentation cheap and easy, so good ideas are identified and implemented.

Final Presentation to the Board or Senior Management

Use the analysis you've recently done and arrange a final document or presentation. If you will present the results to the board, use presentation software (e.g., Keynote, PowerPoint, Prezi) to show your results and request approvals for Game-Changer projects. If you are not presenting to the board, use a simple text document to keep track of results and next steps. As tedious as this step may seem, it's important to wrap things up properly to minimize follow-up questions about what happened.

Give each project a final status update, including:
- whether the project was completed
- what the total costs were
- what the total benefits were
- what the total benefits are expected to be over the next one year and two years
- how Flashpoint 100 will impact the super-objective and junior objectives

You can refer to these records months or years down the line to contrast reality with expectations. Putting this together should be as simple as collecting data from the first and last Pulse Checks.

(See the <u>Final Flashpoint 100 Analysis Template</u> in the back of the book.)

Scenario:

The Flashpoint 100 has been completed, and you are wrapping up the final analysis. You ended the Flashpoint 100 with 10 projects, most of which are completed. After totaling the costs and profits, and you see that you have spent $30,000 as part of the Flashpoint 100, but you have profited $5,000 so far, and will likely benefit another $70,000 over the course of the year.

List of Final Projects, Day 95

#	Name	Function	Project type	Final status	Final cost	Profit to date	Forecast 1 year profit
1	Ml. New Marketing Campaign	Marketing	Meat & Potatoes	Completed	$9,000	$500	$20,000
2	M2. Sponsoring Sports Event	Marketing	Meat & Potatoes	Completed	$2,000	N/A	N/A
3	M3. New High-End Brand	Marketing	Game-Changers	Completed	$5,000	$0	$30,000
4	Sl. Distributor Incentives	Sales	Low-Hanging	Completed	$3,000	$1,000	$5,000
5	S2. Customer Relationship Mgmt System	Sales	Housekeeping	In progress	$500	N/A	N/A
6	Pl. Machine Purchase	Production	Meat & Potatoes	Completed	$10,000	$1,000	$5,000
7	P2. Develop Procurement Process	Production	Housekeeping	Completed	$0	$500	$3,000
8	P3. Develop Production Planning Process	Production	Housekeeping	Completed	$0	N/A	N/A
9	Fl. New Customer Credit Policy	Finance	Low-Hanging	Completed	$0	$2,000	$5,000
10	F2. New Expense Tracking System	Finance	Housekeeping	Completed	$500	$0	$2,000
	TOTAL				$30,000	$5,000	$70,000

Final Presentation to Employees and Final Celebration

Once the board meeting is finished and the final presentation has been given, devote half a day to briefing your employees on what happened, what succeeded, and the next steps. The official post-mortem communication contains lots of review on which projects made it through, and highlights the actions of specific people who made the process go smoothly. If possible, do the same presentation for them that you did for the board, complete with the board's recommendations.

Show your employees the final analysis, including the expected impact of the projects and what it will mean for the company going forward. If specific functions will see major changes, make sure to include that in your analysis. Discuss highlights and stories from Flashpoint 100, from surprising things that happened, to ways employees went above and beyond. If you can, get feedback from customers and read out quotes from them.

Where employees have shown great teamwork and accomplishment, highlight their successes to their peers. Invite function heads and key project champions to speak about their experiences, both positive and negative. Champions of the most successful projects should be included, plus any people who had front-line contact with customers or suppliers, or who played a key role in deals or negotiations. If your customer service is done in-house, ask this team to do a presentation on the effect of customer service and the types of requests and questions they got during this period. It's enlightening for the whole company to hear about the work of other functions and how their counterparts struggled and overcame issues that cropped up along the way. It's also a nice bonding opportunity for employees and a way to identify new areas of common ground.

Do a recognition ceremony and give prizes or awards to employees who really made a difference. Make sure there is a cross-section of employees, from junior to senior. Recognize employees for exceptional efforts, even if their projects did not ultimately succeed. Use information from the final Pulse Check on who really went above and beyond, and get nominations from function heads and managers on who deserves recognition.

Give each person a note to affirm their hard work; handwritten notes are ideal for companies with 50 employees or fewer. If you have many employees, do pre-printed cards, but sign them individually. It may sound like a lot of work, but it means a lot to them and costs next to nothing. You can sign 200 cards while sitting in front of the television at home or even while commuting into work each day, so no excuses.

Lastly, throw a party! Do it in the office if you must, or take everyone out for a celebration. Bring food, drinks, festive decorations, entertainment, and party favors. Show your employees that you really appreciate all their hard work during Flashpoint 100. If location and finances allow, host the party at an offsite location over dinner or lunch.

Chapter 21
Epilogue: What Now?

P hew. It's finally over. After a long meeting filled with intense questions, the board seem satisfied that you were making sound recommendations and they approved your new plans. While most projects are wrapped up, the Game-Changers are just getting started. The time of moving at breakneck speed has passed, and you can now return to normal, but "normal" looks a lot different. The company might be larger, there may be temporary workers or outsourced agencies still finishing projects, and there are probably new ways of doing things. Teething problems with some of the newer systems, processes, projects might still be around.

Getting Back to "Normal"

The first priority is to understand the new normal. The company will not go back to all of its original size and shape, so you'll want to decide on new forms of support. You need to find ways to accommodate new demands on employees without significantly adding costs. To think this through, look at the costs and decide if they are likely to generate additional sales or fulfill the ultimate goal of the company. In other areas, you may have outsourced agencies and temps. If these have helped increase productivity or sales, it may be worthwhile to make the arrangements permanent.

Function by function, look at the existing structure and see what's required to put things back to normal. Alert relevant customers and suppliers to any new changes that might affect them or offer a benefit, such as an automatic invoicing system or a change in payment terms. You can also use this opportunity to highlight to them some of the successes of Flashpoint 100.

Tie off Loose Ends

In some cases, such as the Game Changers and a very small number of others, projects are still ongoing. These might be projects that were unavoidably delayed, re-scoped to become bigger than originally intended, or were more promising than originally expected. At this point, shift focus to getting those projects tied off, even if they don't meet "ideal" outcomes. You will soon need people, resources, and energy elsewhere, so unless the project promises a big payoff, focus on getting the project finished up.

Host Wrap-up Meetings

Host meetings and discussions with project champions and function heads to officially close off Flashpoint 100 and get their feedback on how it went. During this time, thank them for their hard work and support, and mention specifics that impressed you. Communicate how their work will affect the company, and make a commitment to take their work forward, ensuring that it remains a part of how the company does business. This signals that their work was recognized, appreciated, and will be incorporated into current practices.

Capture Lessons Learned

It's likely that there were some big stumbles along the way, and things that everyone would rather forget. Instead of sweeping all of these under the carpet, actively seek out lessons learned from the problem areas and what could have been done differently. Perhaps the suppliers were willing to give discounts if volumes could be guaranteed in advance, or other service providers gave freebies in exchange for referrals. Maybe you learned that customers cared more about on-time delivery than whether the order was right. Other lessons learned may have resulted from technology-related mistakes: like a server getting overloaded if a new software product release and a major customer promotion are executed at the same time. It's worth capturing all of these lessons learned for future reference and to share with the rest of the team.

Decide on the Support Structure for the Company

If the plan has worked, there is a good chance there are new areas, functions, or jobs that need to be filled. So, you will need to ask some questions regarding the new company structure:

- What should be the size and shape?
- How many people will you need on staff?
- What skills will the new staff need?
- Can these new opportunities be made available to existing employees to reward them for their hard work and stimulate their professional development? If so, consider asking for applications for these new roles.

Where temporary workers and outsourcing procedures have been successful, consider keeping these arrangements indefinitely, and hiring permanent staff in place of temps.

> **Scenario:**
> You hired eight temporary workers for Flashpoint 100, mostly in Administration and Sales. Now their contracts are finished, but you want to keep a few. In particular, you noticed that in Sales, the amount of revenue generated per salesperson went up dramatically during Flashpoint 100. Before, each of the 10 salespeople sold about $30,000 of merchandise monthly, but during Flashpoint 100 that went up by $3,000. With the gross profit margin and number of sales people, that equals an additional $10,000 in earnings. The sales manager explains that the increase is due to less time spent by Sales doing administrative tasks such as scheduling client calls, filling out expense forms, or sending out brochures in response to client inquiries. You do a quick calculation and realize that the additional gross profit of $10,000 per month, or $120,000 per year, is worth hiring sales assistants full-time, so you hire two of the administrative temps at a salary of $50,000 each.

Integrate New Employees and Redirect Existing Ones

Sometimes, projects in Flashpoint 100 involve hiring new people. There may be new salespeople, a new insourced function, or additions to existing functions. Integrate new hires into the company with clear explanations of the company's services and expectations of their employment. Brief new hires on the process of Flashpoint 100, and how their role aligns with company goals.

The employees who showed capabilities above and beyond their role were probably motivated and ambitious employees who care about the company and getting results. Identify them and work with their line managers to find ways to address their strengths, including professional development opportunities, training, or mentoring. If their line manager or peers might serve as an obstacle for their upward progress, consider direct mentoring and regular check-ins to give them continued encouragement. Solicit their ideas and feedback on a regular basis. When the time is right, move them into roles that benefit from their results-oriented outlook.

Maintaining Ongoing Benefits from Each Type of Project

Maintaining benefits and healthy habits will vary from project to project. For each, understand how to return to normal without losing the benefits of Flashpoint 100.

Game-Changers

Game-Changers are the one type of project that automatically continues after Flashpoint 100 ends, since the purpose was to identify and validate the Game-Changers as ideas. Afterwards, a lot of work still needs to be done to slot them into place. It's a good idea to form Implementation Teams for each Game-Changer that goes forward. Make these teams cross-functional, and represent the interests of each function that will be affected.

Game-Changers may also require significant changes to the company, such as increases in the capacity of Production or additional production lines. Where employees are unable to finalize the requirements of the Game-Changers, consider hiring outside help like specialists, agencies, or consultants. For example, including a new production line to expand your business from powdered to liquid beverage production may require special consultants for the product design, equipment purchase, production processes, and safety requirements.

Like the project profiles in Flashpoint 100 itself, the ongoing Game-Changers should have clear implementation plans, owners, steps, and timelines. Expect to review progress on a monthly or quarterly basis with senior managers or a board if you have one, and continue monitoring one-on-one on a regular basis with the project champions.

Scenario:
One approved Game-Changer project is opening a new office in a growing market. An Implementation Team was formed from Marketing, Sales, Finance, HR, and Administration. The team's role was to select the site, choose who will open the new office, create a staffing plan of local hires, analyze the costs, contract a lease, and develop the logistics plan. With you, they also agreed on three-month and first-year sales targets, which are used to begin hiring new employees.

Meat and Potatoes Projects

Meat and Potatoes projects are the heart of Flashpoint 100 and will need to be integrated into operations. A large promotional campaign may have brought in many new customers, who now need to be assigned Customer Account Managers. Perhaps a trade conference exhibit created a strong pipeline of leads, requiring Marketing to put together special brochures on a new product package.

Many Meat and Potatoes projects may require ongoing support or changes to the status quo. Others may require additional support or effort during the year, perhaps quarterly or annually, or before a major meeting or conference.

Low-Hanging Fruit Projects

Some of the Low-Hanging Fruit projects were one-offs, and nothing more needs to be done with them. Apart from looking for other one-off opportunities to pursue (an automatic yes if the benefits are clear and guaranteed), many Low-Hanging Fruit projects just need to be monitored for continued benefits. For instance, include pricing discounts from suppliers on each invoice and in the next contract negotiation.

Other Low-Hanging Fruit projects require ongoing attention, such as alternative new financing from credit cards, supplier discounts,

---

inexpensive consultants, or periodically hiring accounts receivable help. Within the appropriate function, assign someone to manage this on an ongoing basis.

Housekeeping Projects

Now that Housekeeping projects are in place, make sure to continue these good habits. Many Housekeeping projects involve doing things in a new way on an ongoing basis that helps the business run better such as regular updates, an invoicing process, or new rules on giving credit to customers. As much as possible, emphasize to employees that these new habits must be integrated into their daily work lives.

If you have been very good at establishing Housekeeping projects, you will see an increase of qualitative benefits, such as better communication, more collaboration, or greater efficiency. Since these gains are due to better habits, remind employees that a more professional company often requires these somewhat tedious processes. If you get a lot of feedback that certain habits or processes are just not working, take that under advisement and consider making changes, while keeping in mind that Housekeeping projects often don't show what is fully at stake. For instance, failing to use a new automated invoicing process can lead to customers paying invoices weeks later than they should. Inefficiencies often bear a hidden cost that can be substantial.

Positioning the Company for Further Growth

Usually Game-Changers make the company bigger. Start making the lower-cost changes now to support the development of Game-Changers and ease this transition. Higher-cost investments, such as purchasing machinery or property or hiring new employees, should be made with the timelines and progress of Game-Changers. Making them too early could mean that you pay too much or they are under-used before the Game-Changer project kicks in. Making them too late could mean that they are not ready when it's time to execute.

Understaffed functions or sections that are operating at or near capacity may need significant changes. If the functions are unlikely to handle much more business without significant changes, consider planning those changes in advance. Decide in advance which triggers should mean increasing resources like adding employees or investing in new equipment. For example, adding a new distribution channel may need a dedicated Customer Service team.

You may also want to re-examine reporting lines and functions. As you introduce new products, perhaps the Supply Chain should be a separate division from Production to better ensure quality, on-time delivery, low cost, and efficiency of inputs. Or perhaps the growth of new customers means that you create a dedicated Accounts Receivable function within Finance, specifically responsible for collecting payment on invoices.

Scenario:
One of the Game-Changers that you approved is to release a new line of flavored iced teas to complement your existing line of juices. You already have a cold-bottling production line for the juices and refrigerated trucks for distribution. But the new line will require a new brand, packaging, supply chain, and production process (the tea must be boiled and then cooled, unlike juices). This will require additional production, distribution, and sales and marketing staff, but they don't need to be added all at the same time.

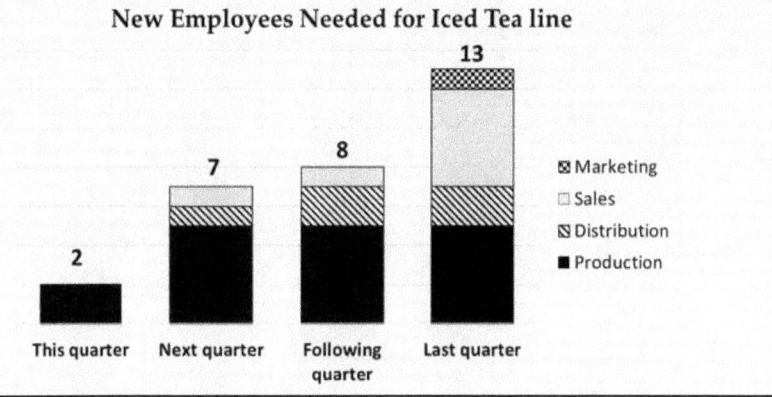

New Employees Needed for Iced Tea line

Looking Ahead

Your company is now more nimble, dynamic, and capable. It's leaner, more cash-efficient, and ready to tackle the challenges the market throws at you. While the going will not be smooth, by returning to the core of Flashpoint 100, you can see your way through any new challenge.

Implementing the Game-Changers may also be a rocky road, but keep the vision of the company in mind, stay the course, and you'll be less likely to go wrong. Flashpoint 100 is a tremendous effort and if you made it this far, you've already won. Learning what motivates employees, how to get the most from the business, how to be efficient with cash, and how to satisfy customers are all valuable gifts that few companies get in such a short period of time.

APPENDIX

Templates

Several steps of Flashpoint 100 require a tracking tool or table of analysis. In this section, you can find the templates for this work, which have been designed to save you time. If you need additional copies, rip out the pages of this book and scan and print. Visit www.Flashpoint100.com for these templates in downloadable/printable form, and for additional support to use them. Or if you prefer, develop your own templates in Microsoft Excel.

Each template section includes a brief description, instructions on how to fill it in, and a blank template. In some cases, you may want to build the template into an Excel or other spreadsheet file to manipulate data more quickly. This is particularly effective for quantitative templates such as the Dashboard, as well as templates that will be repeatedly filled in, such as the Pulse Check and Checkpoint templates.

List of Templates

T1.　Vision and Mission Statements, Company Values, Objectives
T2.　The Company Diagnostic
T3.　Project Breakdown
T4.　Project Profile
T5.　Conversion Metrics
T6.　Total Costs for Flashpoint 100
T7.　Project Analysis: Costs, Earnings, Net Profit
T8.　Pulse Check
T9.　Checkpoint Review
T10.　Dashboard
T11.　 Final Flashpoint 100 Analysis

T1. Vision and Mission Statements, Company Values, and Super- and Junior Objectives

The Vision Statement, Mission Statement, Company Values, and Objectives serve as the operational compass for your business and Flashpoint 100. This template is the most critical; anyone reading it cold should immediately gain an understanding of the business goals and choices you will be making. This is why it is so important.

Instructions

- **Vision Statement**: The Vision statement describes the qualitative vision of the company, painting a clear picture of your ambition.
- **Mission Statement**: The Mission Statement specifies how you will achieve your ambitions.
- **Company Values:** The Company Values section lists the shared beliefs the company has that match the ambition, like transparency, honesty, fairness, sustainability, diversity, etc.

Objectives

Objectives are metrics used to guide you through Flashpoint 100.

- **The super-objective** is the most important metric. It is a big quantitative objective that is consistent with achieving the Vision statement. A good super-objective is easy to measure and cuts across all functions. Common super-objectives relate to total revenues, number of customers, number of units sold, etc.
- **Junior objectives** are a subset of the super-objective. Achieving all the junior objectives should mean achieving

the super-objective as well. Junior objectives can be qualitative or quantitative, and cross-functional or related to just one function.

Vision and Mission Statement, Company Values, and Super- and Junior Objectives

Vision Statement		

Mission Statement		

Company Values		

Objectives		
Super-objective	**Junior Objectives**	
	1	
	2	
	3	
	4	

T2. The Company Diagnostic

The Company Diagnostic is a tool that quickly assesses the business, and allows you to identify metrics that will be tracked later on. Filling out the Company Diagnostic honestly will help you understand where areas of concern or opportunities are so you can get ideas and measure progress during Flashpoint 100.

The Company Diagnostic includes space to assess different parts of the business area (e.g., Products) and a metric that is specific to that part of the business level (e.g., number of products offered). Ideally, the level should be a quantitative metric that allows you to measure the difference later.

Instructions

At a minimum, follow eight metrics related to: volume, revenue, cost of sales, gross margin, fixed costs, cash in the bank, working capital, and earnings, for the last 2 years

- **Financial metrics**

    1. **Volume of units sold**—Depending on your business, this could stand for customers, units, or transactions. Think about what makes the most sense, and what drives the bottom line. If you sell products, choose number of units sold. If you sell subscriptions or bundles of services, consider measuring customers or average bundle sales. If you are in a "two-sided market," where you facilitate transactions between two parties (like eBay), consider using transactions as this metric.

2. **Revenue (sales)**—This standard number reflects the overall size of the company and is usually easy to measure. For Flashpoint 100, use revenues that are promised to the company, even if they're not paid in yet. For example, if you sell $10,000 worth of product on Day 80 but the customer will only pay on Day 110, you can count this revenue toward your goal.

3. **Cost of sales**—These are the costs to make or perform your actual product or service. Include all of the costs that change, depending on how much you make or perform: raw materials, manufacturing costs, distribution costs, shipping costs, sales commissions, etc. Don't include marketing costs, and don't include things that you have to pay regardless of how much you sell, such as electricity, salaries, or rent. For restaurants, cost of sales would include the food, but not the salaries of the wait staff. For many service-based businesses, the cost of sales may be very low, such as travel expenses and printing of meeting materials. If you do not know how much your product or service costs, find out now.

4. **Gross margin ($ and %)**—Gross margin (amount) is the difference between a product's price and its cost. For instance, if you sell a widget for $3.00 but you bought it for $2.00, then your gross margin is $1.00 ($3.00 minus $2.00). To get the percentage divide the margin amount by the price, e.g. $1.00/$3.00 = 33%. Gross margin directly affects your overall profitability, so it's often a good metric to monitor. If your pricing changes, if you offer significant discounts, or if you have different products or services that are priced differently and cost different amounts, your gross margin will be affected.

5. **Fixed costs**—Fixed costs are the costs that don't change regardless of how much you sell. These usually include overheads like rent, salaries, etc. Sometimes these costs are "lumpy" and are paid all at once; for instance, a license fee. To come up with a monthly total fixed cost figure, add up

all your yearly expenses and divide by twelve. For a quarterly figure, do the same but divide by four.

6. **Working capital** — The amount of money that is 'tied up' because you have to pay employees or suppliers before receiving customer payments. Working capital is important because it's the extra money you need to cover your obligations. For instance, if you need to pay suppliers $50,000 for a special order on May 1, but the customer will only pay on July 1, the working capital for this order is $50,000. To find working capital, calculate the extra money needed to make all your required payments before your customers are expected to pay, for a given period (e.g. 4 months, 1 year).

7. **Cash in the bank**—Cash is different from revenues, because it measures what has actually been spent and what has actually been received, not just what is promised. This is important because the faster you get paid by your clients, and the better terms you have from your suppliers, the more cash you have in the bank. With more cash, you can do more projects, or simply manage the business better (e.g., pay employees earlier or get bulk purchase discounts). Monitoring cash is a valuable metric, especially if some of your customers are not good at paying on time or if suppliers require early payment.

8. **Earnings**—Earnings (profit) before taxes or interest on loans is a great way to measure the overall profitability of the business. The formula to calculate earnings is total revenues minus total costs. For the purposes of Flashpoint 100, don't include one-off costs that are associated with Flashpoint 100 itself. These are project costs, and will be calculated separately. You may be spending on unusual things that won't normally reflect the business, such as experiments. However, include recurring expenses like annual license fees.

To calculate the amount of cash that is available for Flashpoint 100, the basic formula looks like this:

> (cash in bank) + (3-4x monthly profit after expenses) − (3-4 months' working capital) = TOTAL MONEY AVAILABLE FOR FLASHPOINT 100

- **Business Model**—The types of customers (consumers, businesses), whether you sell direct to end users or via distributors or resellers, and the way you charge them (monthly subscription, one-off pricing, etc.).
- **Marketplace**—Key suppliers, buyers (for business-to-business). If you are in a heavily regulated market, you include your market restrictions.
- **Competition**—The fierceness of the competition and the number of competitors. How are they competing (e.g., on price), and where is there room for you to do more?
- **Products**—The main products and services that you provide, as well as any "star" features or lines that are underperforming, and product prices. If there are a lot of products and prices, list the biggest ones.
- **Marketing**—The main marketing methods that you use, and how well they perform.
- **Target customers**—Your main customers by attitude or motivation, location, or demographics.
- **Gaining and retaining customers**—How you get new customers (e.g., incentives for new members or referrals), and any retention or loyalty programs.
- **Sales and Distribution**—The basic sales model, whether automated or a sales force. Include methods and materials used for sales and account management. For Distribution, summarize the distribution model, such as insourced or outsourced.
- **Company**—Size and shape of the company, including number of offices/sites, their location, and number of employees in each.

- **Employees**—The number of people who work for you, their functions, and whether you use consultants/contractors or part-time workers.
- **Operations**—How the operations of the company are structured, and how well-defined or automated the processes are. This includes outsourced processes and the manufacturing or production processes.
- **Partners**—Third parties that help the company survive. They might be distributors, outsourcers, marketing partnerships, affiliates, or companies with bilateral agreements in place.
- **Technology and assets**—Trademarks, patents, logos, and licenses that the company has developed or bought, or relies on to function (software, production equipment, vehicles, etc.).
- **Biggest risks**—The biggest potential risks to the company, either internal (e.g., mismanagement or project failure) or external (a lawsuit or a new competitor).
- **Culture**—How people work together and what they value. Company culture is like a personality, with things that work and don't work. Describe cultural strengths or weaknesses. Are people reliable? Entrepreneurial? Are they diligent, creative, collaborative, and/or personally accountable?

The Company Diagnostic, Before Flashpoint 100

Company Diagnostic		
Area	**Description, Strengths and Weaknesses**	**Level**
Financial		Total units sold: Revenues: $ Cost of sales: $ Gross profit: $ Gross profit: % Fixed costs: $ Cash in bank: $ Working capital: $ Total for F100: $

Business Model		
Marketplace		
Competition		
Products		
Marketing		
Target Customers		
Gaining & Retaining Customers		
Sales & Distribution		
Company		
Employees		
Operations		
Partners		
Technology & Assets		
Biggest Risks		
Culture		

The Company Diagnostic, After Flashpoint 100

Company Diagnostic		
Area	**Description of Changes**	**Level**
Financial		Total units sold: Revenues: $ Cost of sales: $ Gross profit: $ Gross profit : % Fixed costs: $ Cash in bank: $ Working capital: $ Total for F100: $
Business Model		
Marketplace		
Competition		
Products		
Marketing		
Target Customers		
Gaining & Retaining Customers		
Sales & Distribution		
Company		
Employees		

Operations		
Partners		
Technology & Assets		
Biggest Risks		
Culture		

T3. Project Breakdown

The Project Breakdown template allows you to see the split of Game-Changers, Meat and Potatoes, Low-Hanging Fruit, and Housekeeping projects. Aim for a high number of Housekeeping and Low-Hanging Fruit Projects, a moderate number of Meat and Potatoes projects, and a small number of Game-Changers.

Instructions

Use the templates included with a calculator, download them from www.Flashpoint100.com, or build the table in Excel. If you're using Excel, copy and paste the Totals table, and use the formulas described below to create sums and percentages.

Totals table
- **Type**: Type of project (Game-Changers, Meat and Potatoes, Low-Hanging Fruit, Housekeeping)
- **Total**: Count by hand, or use the formula "SUM(number1...number2)" in Excel to total all the different projects.
- **Percent (%)**: To create percentages, take the previous column's value and divide it by the total at the bottom of the Total column.

Projects Breakdown table
- **Code**: Project code.
- **Project name**: Name of Project.
- **Project type**: Enter the type of project (e.g., "Low-Hanging Fruit," "Housekeeping.").

Projects Breakdown

Totals		
Type	**Total**	**%**
Game-Changers		
Meat and Potatoes		
Low-Hanging Fruit		
Housekeeping		
Total		100%

Project Breakdown			
#	**Code**	**Project name**	**Project type**
1			
2			
3			
4			
5			
6			
7			
8			
9			
10			
11			
12			
13			
14			
15			
16			
17			
18			
19			
20			

T4. Project Profile Template

The project profile is one of the most of the important templates, since it serves as a roadmap for project execution. The template has been designed to balance precision with efficiency, so it is important to fill out each section, using only enough detail to be clearly understood.

Throughout Flashpoint 100, refer back to the Project Profile to ensure that a project is on track, within budget, and logically aligned to the objectives. Make copies of this to keep on hand, or visit www.flashpoint100.com for copies that can be downloaded and printed.

Instructions
- **Project Code**: Project code.
- **Project Name**: Name of the project.
- **Project Type**: Game-Changer/Meat and Potatoes/Low-Hanging Fruit /Housekeeping (choose one).
- **Junior objectives**: Junior objectives.
- **Purpose**: Rationale for the project (e.g., what it will accomplish and why the benefits are needed).
- **Description**: One or two paragraphs describing the project, with a clear and specific summary of what it does, how long it will take, the key steps, and who will oversee it. It also includes any major assumptions for it to go as planned.

Required information, data, and research to begin execution:
- List, in bullet format, anything that's needed to start the project. This could include market research, regulatory

requirements, or anything else that could affect the project's viability. For example, to do a targeted media campaign designed to raise brand awareness, first you need to know about any poorly performing markets.

Project steps
- **Activities**: A specific, measurable action to be done.
- **Completion Date**: Date by which the action should be finished.
- **Action Owner**: Person responsible for the action. (Note: this does not have to be the project champion.)
- **Status**: How much progress has been made so far: "Not started," "In progress," "Completed/Done," or "Cancelled."

Impact on other functions
- **Function**: List of functions that will be affected by the project.
- **Predicted Impact**: Specific impact on the function (e.g., extra staffing, data backlog, etc.).
- **Notifications/Approvals**: Whether an approval is needed (e.g., legal), or whether a notification is enough (e.g., administrative). Put N/A if there is no impact or if they do not need to be contacted.

Required Resources
- **Resources**: List of resources (new employees, cash, machines, anything costing money or time).
- **Cost - Capex**: Investments into assets or things that build company value (e.g., new machines).
- **Cost - Opex**: The ongoing costs for operations (e.g., salaries).
- **Date Needed**: Date the resource will be needed.
- **Person Responsible**: The person who is in charge of getting the resource.

Benefits
- **Benefits**: List of expected benefits, qualitative or quantitative.

- **Target Level**: For quantitative benefits, the level. For qualitative benefits, describe target (e.g., higher customer satisfaction).
- **Target date:** Date benefits will be fully received.

Project Profile Template

Project Code: **Project Name:**

Type of Project: Game-Changer/Meat and Potatoes/Low-Hanging Fruit /Housekeeping (choose one)

Junior Objectives:

Purpose:

Description:

Required information, data, and research to begin execution

Project Steps

#	Activity	Completion Date	Action owner	Status
1				
2				
3				
4				

Impact on other functions

#	Function	Predicted impact	Notifications/ Approvals
1			
2			
3			
4			

Required resources

#	Resources	Cost: Capex	Cost: Opex	Date Needed	Person responsible
1					
2					
3					
4					

Benefits

#	Benefit	Target level	Target date
1			
2			
3			
4			

T5. Conversion Metrics

Conversion metrics convert all profit-related values into profit, allowing you to compare apples to apples. You can then sum the profit potential each of the projects. In this case, convert everything to earnings, which reflects the business revenues minus all the business costs. Although it's not a perfect measure, it allows a common standard for each project. This template is a powerful tool for knowing the total profit of Flashpoint 100. Once earnings are calculated, you can then subtract project costs to see the full benefit of the program (net profit).

As the following metrics described, earnings percentage is the proportion of revenue that go to profit.

The formula for earnings percentage is:
(Total revenues - Total costs) ÷ Total revenues = Earnings

Instructions

- **Metric**: What will be converted into earnings equivalent?
- **Description**: An explanation of the metric.
- **Explanation of conversion**: Explanation of how the conversion from the metric into earnings works.
- **Conversion to Earnings**: The formula for converting the relevant inputs into earnings.
- **Total value from Flashpoint 100**: This is the number to convert into earnings. For instance, if you are converting from revenue, this is your revenue number. If you are converting from costs, it's the cost number. If you are converting from new customers, it's the number of new customers and the average revenue per customer.
- **Earnings equivalent**: The final value, once you have converted everything into earnings.

TABLE OF CONVERSION METRICS

Metric	Description	Explanation of conversion	Conversion formula to earnings	Values to be converted	Earnings equivalent
Earnings %	The proportion of each sale that your company keeps as profit after all costs and expenses have been paid	Earnings is calculated as a proportion of revenues, and expressed as a percentage (%)	(Revenues- Total costs) / Revenues		%
New customers	Additional customers that you sell to for the first time	Average number of purchases a customer makes in a year, multiplied by the average order size, multiplied by the earnings %.	Avg. # customer purchases x average order size x earnings %		$
Unit sold	A single sale of a good or service	The earnings amount from each unit sold. If you have many products, use averages.	Unit price x earnings %		$
Revenue increase	Additional sales, income, or revenue, measured in currency (e.g., US$)	Multiply the earnings % times the additional revenue	Earnings % x revenue increase		$

TABLE OF CONVERSION METRICS

Metric	Description	Explanation of conversion	Conversion formula to Earnings	Values to be converted	Earnings equivalent
Cost reduction	Reductions in your operating costs, or in the unit cost to produce something	Cost reductions automatically increase the amount of earnings at 100% of the cost reduction	– Cost reductions x 100% (operating costs) – Cost reductions x 100% x # of units (unit costs)		$
Price increase	Increase in the average price per unit	Price increases (difference between new and old prices) increase earnings at 100% of the difference if new costs aren't involved. Multiply the price increase by the number of units sold. If you have many products, use the average price increase.	Price increase x number of units sold		$
TOTAL					$

T6. Total Costs for Flashpoint 100

Flashpoint 100 requires significant investment. The costs are typically divided into two buckets: opex and capex.

Opex is operating expenditure, or the costs related to ongoing operations like rent, salaries, marketing costs, etc. For this table, include only the increase in operating expenses, such as new hires, new marketing expenses, or new supplier contracts.

Capex is the capital expenditure related to company investments that increase the value of the company such as buildings, vehicles, machinery, or equipment. Typically, these expenses are not made on a regular basis. Include the expenses that are part of Flashpoint 100.

Instructions:
Use the table here and a calculator, download the template from www.Flashpoint100.com, or create this table in Excel. Make sure that the Year 1 and Year 2 columns sum up the previous Quarter columns.
- Capex: The total capital expenditure due to Flashpoint 100.
- Opex: The total operating expenditure INCREASE due to Flashpoint 100.
- Total costs: Sum of opex + capex.

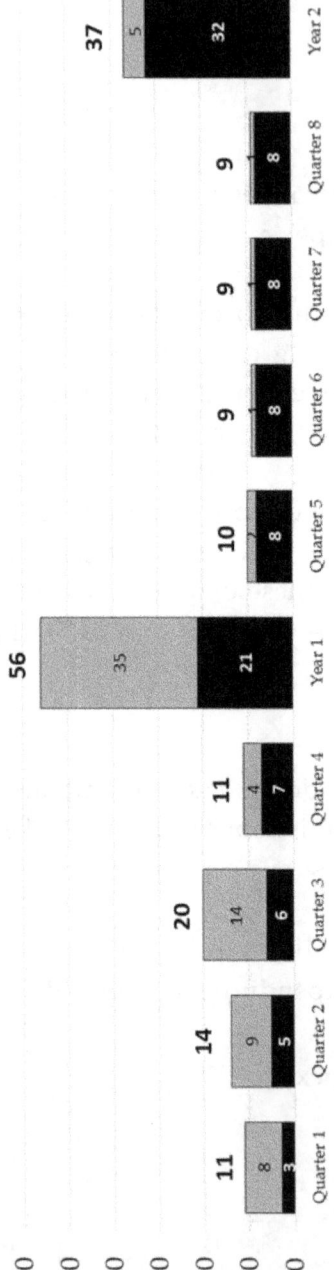

Total costs, opex and capex

Total Costs, Opex and Capex

	Quarter 1	Quarter 2	Quarter 3	Quarter 4	*Year 1*	Quarter 5	Quarter 6	Quarter 7	Quarter 8	*Year 2*
Opex										
Capex										
Total costs										

T7. Project Analysis: Costs, Earnings, Net Profit

The Project Analysis allows you to quickly sum up the changes from Flashpoint 100. In reality, many projects will not be completed, so the amount of earnings is just illustrative at this point. It does show you whether the total Flashpoint 100 is worthwhile from a net profit perspective, and whether the expected benefits will justify all the time, effort, action, and costs.

Instructions

Summary Table
Link the summary table to the project costs, profit, and net profit as outlined below. Once it's finished, you can build a chart with the data and display the results.

- **Project total costs (During Flashpoint 100/First Year/First 2 Years)**: link to Totals column in table below.
- **Project earnings (During Flashpoint 100/First Year/First 2 Years)**: link to Totals column in table below.
- **Project net profit (During Flashpoint 100/First Year/First 2 Years)**: link to Totals column in table below.

Project Costs, Profit, and Net Profit:

- **Code**: Project code.
- **Name**: Project name.
- **Project total costs (During Flashpoint 100/First Year/First 2 Years)**: Total project costs for the duration of Flashpoint 100, the first year, and the first two years. Include both capex and opex, but ONLY project-related costs.

- **Project earnings (During Flashpoint 100/First Year/First 2 Years):** Total profit from Flashpoint 100, based on converting the revenues and cost savings to earnings. Do this for the first three months, the first year, and the first two years.
- **Project net profit (During Flashpoint 100/First Year/First 2 Years):** Subtract the project costs from the project earnings to get the net profit, which reflects the amount left after the projects have been completed.

Project Costs, Earnings, and Net Profit

Projects Financial Summary			
Name	3 months	First year	First 2 years
Project total costs			
Project earnings			
Project net profit			

Project Costs, Earnings, and Net Profit

#	Code	Name	Department	During Flashpoint 100			First Year			First 2 Years		
				Project total costs	Project earnings	Project net profit	Project total costs	Project earnings	Project net profit	Project total costs	Project earnings	Project net profit
1												
2												
3												
4												
5												
6												
7												
8												
9												
10												
TOTAL												

T8. Pulse Check

The Pulse Check is a weekly meeting to check progress on specific projects. Hold this meeting with the project champions of each ongoing project, whether or not the project is going well. Do it face-to-face if possible so that you can pick up on any issues or problems early on. Using this template during the meeting will help you keep track of the project's progress. Make additional copies, or visit www.flashpoint100.com for copies you can download and print.

Instructions

- **Project, Project champion, Meeting with, Date**: Name and code of project, name of project champion, name of person you are meeting, date of the meeting.
- **Which Pulse Check this is**: Circle the number of pulse checks this will be, from 1 to 12.
- **Notes**: How the meeting went, any challenges, any noteworthy events, and any risks that might affect progress.
- **Status**: Circle whether the project is on track, off track, or not applicable.
- **Next Steps**: Things that need to happen in the project.
- **Decision**: Circle whether the project should proceed, be cancelled, or be delayed (stopped).

Financials
- **Total allocated**: Money allocated to the project, based on the Project Profile.
- **Total spent**: Amount actually spent on the project.
- **Total remaining**: Amount of money remaining, based on Total Allocation minus Total Spent.

Pulse Check Template
(To fill out during meeting)

Project   : _____

Project Champion : _____

Meeting with   : _____

Date   : _____

Which Pulse Check is this? 1 2 3 4 5 6 7 8 9 10 11 12 *(circle one)*

Status: On Track/Off Track/Not Applicable *(choose one)*

Notes:

Next Steps:

FINANCIALS
    Total allocated:
    Total spent:
    Total remaining:

Decision: Proceed/Cancel/Delay *(choose one)*

T9. Checkpoint Review Template

The Checkpoint Review Template allows you to review *all* of the projects in aggregate, based on their Checkpoint meetings, so that you can analyze the progress of Flashpoint 100 and make any necessary changes. The template gives a high-level view of the process overall, areas of common problems, areas of success, and the total number of projects in progress.

The Checkpoint Totals table gives a view of the projects' financials so that you can better monitor the amount of money spent so far, future amounts you plan to spend, and the likely financial impact.

Instructions

- **Date:** Date of the review meeting.
- **Total Projects to be reviewed:** Total number of projects to be reviewed for decisions.
- **General review of the process:** One paragraph on how well Flashpoint 100 is going; are people working together well? Are projects progressing as expected? Are the milestones appropriate?
- **Common benefits:** One paragraph on where things are going really well, for example, by function, type of project, type of people, etc.
- **Common problems:** One paragraph on ongoing problems across projects, and ideas for improvements.

Table
- **Function:** Which function the project comes from.
- **Code:** Project code.

- **Project:** Project name.
- **Project type:** Game-Changer, Meat & Potatoes, Low-Hanging Fruit, or Housekeeping
- **Status:** On Track/Off Track/Not Applicable.
- **Recommended action**: Choose whether project should Proceed/Cancel/Delay/Increase.
- **Total allocated:** Original total allocated to the project.
- **Total spent:** Amount spent so far.
- **Total remaining:** What's remaining, from Total Allocated minus Total Spent.
- **Total to be given:** Recommended amount to be given in this round, based on upcoming milestones.
- **Notes:** Any notes on the projects, including whether they should be re-scoped, scaled up, or changed.

Checkpoint Review Template
(To fill out during meeting)

Date:
Total Projects to Be Reviewed:

General review of the process:

Common benefits:

Common problems:

Checkpoint Totals

#	Department	Code	Project	Project type	Status	Recommended action	Total allocated	Total spent	Total remaining	Total to be given	Notes
1							$	$	$	$	
2							$	$	$	$	
3							$	$	$	$	
4							$	$	$	$	
5							$	$	$	$	
6							$	$	$	$	
7							$	$	$	$	
8							$	$	$	$	
9							$	$	$	$	
10							$	$	$	$	
TOTAL							$	$	$	$	

T10. Dashboard

The Dashboard provides a snapshot of the projects that are underway. It includes a view of all projects and their status (e.g., on track, off track, delayed, cancelled), as well as an aggregate view of Flashpoint 100 as a whole, complete with financials. This is best when built in Excel so that charts can be created. Sample charts appear below the template.

Instructions

After building this table in Excel, use the Chart function to produce charts that summarize the information.

Summary

- **Date:** Today's date.
- **Total number of ongoing projects:** Total open projects.
- **Total spent:** Total money that has been spent on projects, to date.
- **Total remaining:** Total money that has been allocated but not spent, to date.
- **Earnings:** Earnings so far (profit resulting from doing Flashpoint 100).
- **Net Profit:** Remaining profit after subtracting the total that's been spent on the projects themselves.
- **Common benefits:** Areas that are working well.
- **Common problems:** Areas that are consistently causing issues in the process.

Status

- **Project:** Project name
- **Project Type:** Game-Changer, Meat & Potatoes, Low-Hanging Fruit, or Housekeeping
- **Function:** Function of project champion
- **Status:** On track, Off track, Delayed, Cancelled

Projects

- **Number of Game-Changers Projects**: Total number of Game-Changer projects, by function.
- **Number of Meat and Potatoes Projects**: Total number of Meat and Potatoes projects, by function.
- **Number of Low-Hanging Fruit Projects**: Total number of Low-Hanging Fruit projects, by function.
- **Number of Housekeeping Projects**: Total number of Housekeeping projects, by function.
- **Total number of projects**: Sum of the previous four columns, by function.

Financials

- **Costs - Total allocated**: Total allocated for projects, from the Project Profile.
- **Costs - Total spent**: Total spent on projects.
- **Costs - Total remaining**: Total allocated less total spent on projects.
- **Benefits - Gross Profit**: The Gross Profit, calculated as revenues minus cost of sales. Does not allow for non-product costs such as salaries, rent, or advertising.
- **Benefits - Cost redux**: Cost reductions from non-product costs such as salaries or rent.
- **Benefits - Earnings**: Earnings is gross profit + cost redux.
- **Benefits - Net Profit**: Net profit after project costs, calculated as earnings minus total spent.

Dashboard

Date   : _____

Total number of ongoing projects : _____

Total spent   : _____

Total remaining   : _____

Earnings   : _____

Net Profit   : _____

Common benefits	Common problems

Project	Project Type	Function	Status

Projects and Financials									
Projects					**Financials**				
	Number of projects				**Costs**			**Benefits**	
Department	Game-Changers	Meat & Potatoes	Low-Hanging Fruit	House-keeping	*Total projects*	Total allo-cated	Total spent	*Total remaining*	Gross Profit	Cost redux	*Earnings Net Profit*

Example Charts You Can Build from
www.Flashpoint100.com or in Excel

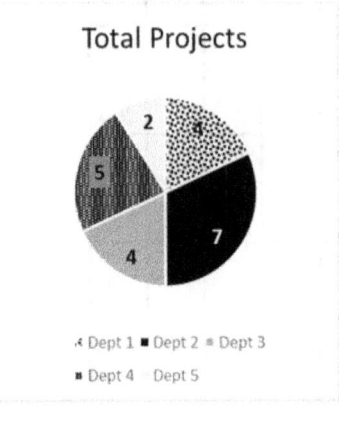

Total Projects

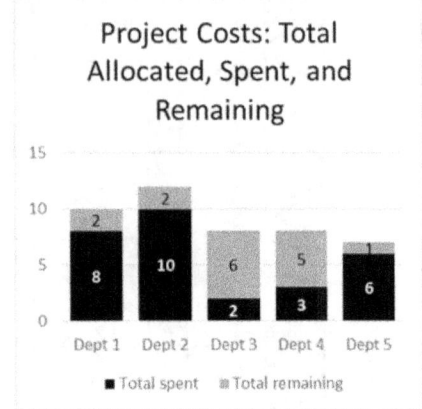

T11. Final Flashpoint 100 Analysis

The final analysis for Flashpoint 100 allows you to see its impact and justify your efforts to employees and the board of directors or investors, if applicable. It also provides valuable insight into employee collaboration and the types of projects they are good at executing. The analysis contains both qualitative and quantitative reviews, so you can see the impact of what worked.

Instructions
Process Analysis
For the Process Analysis, fill in with one- or two-sentence answers for every question
- **Question:** Area of the process to be reviewed
- **Result:** One- to two-sentence review of that area of the process

Project Analysis
- **Function:** Function being analyzed
- **Projects started:** Total number of projects started on Day 15, by function
- **Projects completed:** Total number of projects completed (or near completion) on Day 95, by function
- **Superstar project champions:** Any project champions from the function that deserve special recognition for their efforts or accomplishments

Qualitative benefits analysis
For the Process Analysis, fill in one- to two- sentence answers for every question
- **Area:** Area of the qualitative benefit to be reviewed

- **Result:** One- to two-sentence review of that area

List of Final Projects

The list of final projects is used as a final snapshot for Flashpoint 100 so it's clear which projects were completed, and which are still ongoing (keep these to a minimum).

- **Code:** Project code.
- **Name:** Project name.
- **Function:** Function heading up the project.
- **Project type:** Game-changer, Meat and Potatoes, Low-Hanging Fruit, Housekeeping.
- **Final status:** Ongoing or done.
- **Final cost:** Total spent on the completed projects. For ongoing projects, note the amount spent so far.
- **Profit to date:** Include the earnings realized so far, calculated as the profit minus the project costs.
- **Forecast one-year profit:** Based on conservative estimates of growth on profits realized thus far, estimate a reasonable expectation of the profit for the year.

The Final Flashpoint 100 Analysis

Project Analysis			
Function	Projects started	Projects completed	Superstar project champions

Qualitative Benefits Analysis

Area	Review	Examples
Professionalism		
Communication		
Collaboration		
Alignment		
Information capture, storage, and use		

The Process Analysis

Question	Result
Did people work together well? Or did they compete and withhold information or support?	
Did people go above and beyond their usual level of effort?	
Where was the planning insufficient or inappropriate?	
Where was money, time, or effort wasted?	
Who surprised you with what they were able to accomplish?	
Who disappointed you with what they did not get done?	
Where was the process too ambitious?	
How much extra time did the staff spend working?	
Which types of projects did especially well?	

Quantitative Analysis- List of Final Projects, day 95

#	Code	Name	Department	Project type	Final Status	Final cost	Profit to date	Forecast 1-year profit
1						$	$	$
2						$	$	$
3						$	$	$
4						$	$	$
5						$	$	$
6						$	$	$
7						$	$	$
8						$	$	$
9						$	$	$
10						$	$	$
	TOTAL					$	$	$

Index